Handwriting Analysis Made Easy

John Marley

Melvin Powers
Wilshire Book Company

12015 Sherman Road, No. Hollywood, CA 91605

First published and
Copyright © 1967
by Bancroft & Co.
(Publishers) Ltd.
Greencoat House, Francis Street
London SW 1
Manufactured in the United States of America

ISBN 0-87980-045-3

CONTENTS

'A man may lie, simulate, disown himself: a portrait may change or beautify him: a book can lie and so can a letter, but in one thing man is inseparably attached to the innermost truth of his nature—in his handwriting. Handwriting betrays a man, whether he wants it or not, it is as unique as his personality, and sometimes reveals what he conceals. Although handwriting does not betray everything, it does reveal the essential—the essence of personality, as it were, is given in a tiny abbreviation.'

Stefan Zweig
Sunday Times Book Exhibition
London

Foreword

OF all the inventions of man, one of the most outstanding has undoubtedly been handwriting, enabling him to record and communicate his thoughts and ideas. This book is an introduction to graphology, a science whereby man can analyse and evaluate handwriting through a set pattern of principles and so ascertain the personal qualities of the writer. In general most people are ignorant of the functions of the graphologist and may view the work with some suspicion and even doubt. They may place him in the same category as a seer, or confuse him with a handwriting expert who specializes in Court work. As an introduction this work seeks to activate and to stimulate a much wider interest in this science. It aims to bring within the scope of the average reader a new avenue of thought, a new interest and insight into human relationships, whether it be husband and wife, parent and child, employer and employee, in fact wherever human beings meet and make contact throughout the world.

This book will endeavour to explain in the simplest possible terms a method of assessment whereby, through the graphic motion of handwriting, basic characteristics can be observed with outstanding clarity, just as mannerisms can be detected when meeting a person for the first time. We assess a person on voice, eyes, handshake, and a multitude of other observations, so that we believe that we 'know' this person. Yet we may not know him at all; we may only know the outer shell—the veneer. In fact we have the capacity to like and to dislike, sometimes without knowing the true reason. We can feel that we are uneasy with a person, that there is an 'atmosphere'. We are unable to understand this feeling, but we are very much aware of it. Wherever there are doubts, this modern scientific method of analysing handwriting can assist us to understand the reason why we clash, why there is an atmosphere, why we feel uneasy.

We have the ability through handwriting analysis to remove the mask and to see the true person who has projected himself unconsciously on to a blank page; who has painted a word portrait of himself, who has expressed his true personality; and has revealed his temperament, his constitution and the foundation of the whole character structure. All is revealed. Thus with this additional information, plus our gauged opinion on outer impact and normal assessment, we can build up a more complete character portrait which enables us to assess even the most complicated and difficult of persons who may cross our path during the course of our life. This book has been titled 'Simple Graphology'. It does not aim to enter the field of the highly technical books on the subject; but it does aim to present itself as a book within a wide field of general understanding, where the average man or woman can have some knowledge of the subject and with reasonable care can be able to assess the basic traits in the character structure which would otherwise have been hidden from view in the normal course of meeting. Just as there are no two finger prints completely alike and no two faces alike, so there are no two handwritings completely alike. There can be similarities, but what are known as *basic dominants* (these appear in all forms of handwriting) are the matter with which we are most concerned.

It is hoped that this little book will allow the reader to embark on a new voyage of discovery, this time into the workings of the human mind unconsciously betrayed in handwriting on to a plain piece of paper. Just as the artist paints a portrait of a person on to a canvas, so the writer paints a portrait of himself with his handwriting.

History of Graphology

IF we look back to our early ancestors we find the tracings of rudimentary pictorial and graphic signs in caves. Just as a young child of today endeavours to draw before he can write, so in very early times these signs can be assumed to be an attempt at writing: a means to communicate. But the overall development during the course of centuries was extremely slow in evolving a formed and established alphabet; and it was not until the Phoenicians produced the first alphabetical signs that we can say writing (as we know it today) had first begun to be used.

The Greeks in turn adopted the alphabet and provided additional signs to represent vowels, at the same time they changed the direction of writing from right to left as used by Semitic peoples, and redirected it from left to right. In the course of colonization the Greeks handed over their alphabet to the Etruscans who adopted it for their own use; they in turn, when under the Roman influence, found this alphabet accepted and absorbed by the Romans. After modifications it was finally stabilized as the alphabet we know today. The capitals are almost identical but the small letters have had considerable modification. The Latin form of script spread rapidly on account of its clear, simple and positive outlines.

It can be said that throughout history handwriting has interested many observers: as early as the 2nd century C.Suetonius Tranquillus noted the pecularities of the handwriting of Caesar, whilst in the 11th century the Chinese had also noted the relationship between handwriting and personality.

In Europe until the 12th century handwriting was almost entirely limited to monks, whose work on manuscripts was more a thing of ornamentation and beauty than a fluid means of communication; and it was inevitable that the knowledge of handwriting could not be kept forever within the confines of the monasteries; and therefore it began to spread outside the monastery walls and became part of the natural line of communication. Although the teaching of the alphabet—the formation of words, spelling etc.,—was made originally by the monks, it was noted almost at once, that there was an individualistic trend being shown by every writer and this caused a certain doctor and professor at the University of Bologna—named Camillo Baldi—to write a book entitled '*The means of knowing the habits and qualities of a writer from his letters*'. This was published in the 17th century, in the year 1622. As far as can be ascertained during the 18th century no major interest was displayed towards such observations, but by the mid–19th century a very significant development occurred.

A group of French clergy began to examine the possible relationship between handwriting and personality. Amongst this group was a man by the name of the Abbé Flandrin, who was the teacher of the Abbé Jean Hippolyte Michon.

Jean Hippolyte Michon not only coined the name 'graphology' but went ahead with research in this field and published in Paris in 1872 a book under the title *The Mysteries of Handwriting* and a further book entitled *A System of Graphology*. These two books created a sensation as they were the first proof that here was a science that could bear investigation—could be used and could be proved by a wide circle of observers. Michon who had with the help of Flandrin laid the foundation for further research was followed by another Frenchman by the name of J.Crepieux-Jamin who then commenced to develop, modify and elaborate the study from his own observations; and he can be called, with all justification, the 'father of graphology' in the French school.

J.Crepieux-Jamin classified handwriting into seven categories and a hundred and seventy-five specimens which are still in use by graphologists today. He published many works which have remained classics. The original French development was naturally followed by others but like all systems that are empirical they can be debated, altered, condemned and sometimes destroyed. But graphology was fortunate in arousing intense interest on the Continent in its early stages, particularly in Germany where Dr. Ludwig Klages founded the theoretical school, and Robert Saudek continued research in Czechoslovakia, together with Max Pulver in Switzerland, and Schwiedland and Langenbruch in Austria. Strange as it may seem with all this progress and development, very little of the subject was generally known in Great Britain. With the exception of a few highly trained specialists, it was only when a considerable number of Continental graphologists sought asylum in this country at the time of the Nazi period, that books of a general nature were produced and published and contacts made with persons who could see the value of this method of character assessment. Due to the conservative nature of the British, the general pattern of development differed vastly from the Continent. Throughout the country, graphologists carried on their work in comparative secrecy, frowning on any form of advertising and building up their practices rather like doctors and barristers. They respected the fact that it was a highly confidential service, intimate, and with so many avenues whereby the system could be used. Today there is vast publicity being given to graphology on the Continent – in Western Germany alone there are over 2,000 practising graphologists, openly advertising, and nine universities teaching the subject. Also in the United States there is the formation of a vast network of graphologists under the International Graphoanalysts Society. But without doubt Europe is in the forefront in this field. It would appear that we have lagged behind, but this is not the case. Societies have been formed and are being formed, but each individual graphologist still maintains his own confidential circle of clients, earning respect for the science which it justifiably deserves amongst the new techniques used for analysing and assessing character.

The history of graphology must continue, and perhaps the very simplicity of those early findings of Michon, Flandrin and Crepieux-Jamin will find a reflection in the ordinary man and woman, who seek to understand the methods of graphology to be explained in this book, and perhaps in turn through intuition and perception and a particular *sense or feeling* for this work, they may produce and advance their own theories and findings, and so add to the accumulative effect of establishing without doubt the true value of this science.

The whole story is just like something out of a novel — he has lots of things to tell you and wants some advice on when to do next. At the moment he has a fortnight

1 (above): Feminine man

Aged 27: Unmarried. Independent. Designer. Sociable. Obstinate. Desire to control own sphere of influence. Intelligent. Individualist. Deep concentration. Can enlarge on small matters. Observant. Realistic and practical. Good judgment.

Group B

2 (below): Masculine woman

Aged 41. Married. Strong personality. Controls husband and family. Takes great responsibility. Leader type. Firm. Determined. Positive. Protective. Problem solver. Logical. Can enlarge on small matters. Moods. Likes to have own way. Inquiring mind.

Group B

P.S.

Confidentially Betty did as you advised + wrote the letters.

Paul — it may be she has it but I be tied up with American referential of the firm. Hope she sees him before the weekend otherwise his margin a bad spell.

Not Saturday Ger other jours.

How you can use Graphology in your daily life

To become a good graphologist and to use graphology in his daily life requires the student to maintain a very high standard of physical and mental health..It is necessary to be always optimistic, unbiased, clearminded and never to 'imagine' anything about a person when looking at the handwriting, or to 'read in' something which cannot be proved by scientific application. The use of graphology in one's daily life can produce a considerable number of people who are only too interested to have their own handwriting analysed, or to produce some other person's handwriting which they would like analysed. The number of questions and requests that will be asked will be endless once friends and acquaintances get to know that you are involved in the study of graphology. The main thing to do is not to tell anyone you have taken up the study for some considerable time; and to realise that the knowledge you obtain from handwriting must always be treated as confidential.

Very little equipment is necessary. Two magnifying glasses, which can be purchased from any good optician, size 3 to $3^{1}/_{2}$ inches diameter, approximately 20 cm focal length, 2 × magnification: this is an instrument with a handle attached to the lens. The second glass of the pocket variety about 1 to $1^{1}/_{2}$ inches diameter, approximately 10 cm focal length, 4 × magnification. Both these items are necessary and should always be used when analysing. One very important factor to remember with any specimen of handwriting being analysed is *always* to ask the sex, age and nationality of the writer. It is no use guessing as one can be so easily wrong in such an assessment.

We have feminine men who write like women, see specimen (1) and we have masculine women who write like men, see specimen (2). The question of age must always be considered carefully. The best way to approach this problem of age is to explain fully the necessity of knowing the correct age. Some people can at the age of 50 write like children of 16 whilst children of 16 can write like adults of 30 – so on these two vital points one must always inquire. Specimens (3), (4) and (5) overleaf explain this point. If one is honest and one looks directly into the eyes of the person who has presented the handwriting, and if one approaches the problem seriously, then no exception is ever taken over age; in fact one gets full co-operation usually from everyone. It is only necessary to say: "Before I analyse this handwriting I must know the age and sex of the writer", or a sentence similar to this. No more is required. Once more, never start to analyse handwriting until these two vital pieces of information are known. When handwriting is sent through the post for analysis again insist on this information before commencing.

So now armed with the two magnifying glasses, one commences to build up a dossier of handwriting specimens. The best method is to purchase from a good stationers a scrap book. These books are usually bound in substantial covers and can be kept in perfect condition. There must be no slackness in building up the dossier as this is to be the foundation of the study. A very good time to start this collection of specimens is at Christmas time when the steady and endless flow of Christmas cards come through the door.

Most envelopes are written in a very 'natural' manner and are very reliable for using as a test. However if one can obtain a letter, this is much better, for the more handwriting that one can work on the more chance there is of fully ascertaining the character. Now assuming that every card, letter or envelope is from a 'known person', the specimen should then be stuck in the scrap book and either below or on the opposite page a full report should be written on the character of the person concerned. Every known facet. For example:—

'Mr. John Brown. Aged approximately 50. British. Short. Dark. Rather shy and retiring. Cautious. Controlled by his wife. Not a conversationalist. Looks overweight. Never looks healthy. Seems depressed. Employed as manager of local store, could never imagine him as sales type. Reads a lot. Kind and considerate but seems to lack drive. Keen gardener. Likes walking but always seems tired. Appears to worry. Children like him. Never looks at one directly in the eye. This could be shyness. Seemed to like life in army always talks about his past experiences, seems to be only topic that interests him. Likes war films. Feel he lives in a world of dreams. Wife over-powering, dominant. Hope when I study graphology shall know more about him. Would like to help him. Feel there is something submerged in the character.'

This is the type of explanation to give. It can be much longer according to the person. One further example:—

'Mrs. Jane Smith. Age 55. Irish.
Older than husband. Alive. Alert. Likes to have own way. Always cheerful. Always in hurry. Vibrant. Quick talker. Likes doing things. Organizing. Chairwoman of Townswomen's Guild. Fond of fêtes and

bazaars. Very extroverted. Sharp tongue. Has temper. Can be critical. Feels she is born leader. Was manageress of shoe shop once. Very good. She can be very secretive when it comes to herself and family. Likes to control others. Wants to have her own business. Often talks about it. One cannot help liking her. Very friendly. Healthy. Husband keen outdoor man. Think they are good pair.'

Of course these are only brief remarks and much more can be written, but this dossier is vital .for using later on with 'test analyses'. One can keep all the males in one file and all the females in another. One can keep all the upright looking handwriting together, all the sloping handwriting, to either left or right, together: in fact the method of keeping this dossier is purely a matter of individualistic approach. The more specimens obtained the better. One can never have too many. Another good way of obtaining specimens of well-known and important people is to write to them a letter that will produce a reply. In most cases one only obtains a signature—but this will be of considerable use later for analytic purposes. In fact no specimen of handwriting is ever wasted for inclusion in the dossier.

It is felt that children's handwriting should be kept separately and if possible specimens covering say three of four years included for watching the maturity angle and development. Parents who take up this subject should keep one letter a month if the child is away at school as a personal record of progress marking carefully the date and age. If the child is at home a specimen from a notebook should be kept. So much can be learned from this method and the information obtained will prove itself to be of the greatest value in understanding the mood variations and general overall development.

Having begun the dossier (once more it should be emphasized that Christmas is one of the very best times to collect every possible specimen), the 'known' qualities of the writers are entered—the sex and the age. The greater the information entered the better it will be for later probing and reference purposes.

In some cases students of graphology have divided their dossiers into the following groups:—

(a) Husbands and wives.

(b) Parents and children.

(c) Boy and girl friends.

(d) Employers and employees.

These subdivisions are often designed to make comparisons in the field of compatibility. Indexes should be kept and the pages numbered for reference purposes. Where exceptional and outstanding traits are noted, such as leadership, organizing ability and judgment, creativeness, artistic inclinations, inventiveness; in fact all those who have outstanding ability in one way and another should be carefully noted. Scientists, 'boffins' and those in the advanced creative fields should be kept separately, also those who hold high position in industry, or as servants of the State. It is a good method to keep a special scrap book with the handwriting of the 'famous'; this can be of great value and assistance when dealing with the 'top groupings'.

The title of this chapter is 'How to use graphology in your daily life'—it is a wide title—and depends largely on how one is disposed to use the study. Some use it for private purposes—many business executives have made a special study and use their knowledge daily in dealing with staff. Others use it for dealing with children at school, teachers and headmasters: they keep records of handwriting of children showing exceptional promise, they use their knowledge of handwriting in preparing their personal reports, to embellish the normal remarks.

The student who takes up graphology for just the pleasure and interest can in some cases take it up professionally later by building up a circle of people who have not only found its value, but use it on every occasion that warrants investigation. In fact the use of graphology in one's daily life possesses so many opportunities that one can never be dull or bored. A certain amount of time should be set aside for the study daily; and if two or three people are interested, a study 'circle' can become a very pleasant and absorbing interlude. Study circles can be built up and these can become social events.

Finally, the use of graphology in one's daily life is dependent on the person reading this book. How, when and where to use it is the question but the following fairly wide range of usage is outlined below:—

Personnel Selection
Personnel matching for harmonious working
Vocational Guidance
Personnel matching for overseas clients
Marriage Compatibility
Child Guidance   Forgeries
Personality Assessment   Anonymous letters
Analysis of handwriting on historical documents

have arrived at the
... place imaginat
most beautiful; Kin
... family possib
an extraordinarily
On my arrival

3: Mature young person

Female. Aged 16. Independent. Mature. Intelligent.
Realistic. Practical. Individualistic. Good imagination. Deep concentration. Intuitive. Perceptive.
Could be secretive. Thoughtful. Can make and take
decisions. Uses calculation and strategy. Leader
type.
Group B

interested in er
uch as I am in
... home lately
'en like to dabble

of to refer to.
the past we t
d to rely on ou
- thoughts and
lings, and alas.
ogress has been
w - due to lack
owledge.

4: Immature old person

Female. Aged 40. Conscientious. Steady. Sensitive. Disciplined. Simplicity of outlook. Non-complicated group. Kind and considerate. Lacks deep maturity and intelligence. Purity of thought. Can enlarge on small matters. More diplomatic than friendly. Open on surface but could be secretive. Intuitive.

Group D

5 (left): Immature old person

Male Aged 51. Mechanic. Excellent workman on practical side. Open. Friendly. Nervous. Has had serious nervous breakdown. Simplicity of outlook. Rather lost. Lacks firmness. Shows uncertainty as to way he is going. Very reserved. Gets depressed. Lacks educational background. Good planning mind in the practical field. Wife intelligent.

Group E

How to assess handwriting on impact and to establish its form level

As we meet people we pick up vibrations, consciously or subconsciously. Like or dislike. So with handwriting. We pick up vibrations. Known or unknown. Like or dislike. Impressed or unimpressed. Genuine or not genuine. Natural or artificial as per specimens (6) and (7). Every facet in the word portrait of the writer strikes on impact. Often one hears the remark, 'he has terrible handwriting' or 'you should see the handwriting of my doctor', or 'I have never seen such beautiful handwriting'. But our reaction on impact is positive, we are aware that something has struck us most forcibly. It is as though we have seen a picture we admire—or dislike. Then on second thoughts as we examine the workmanship we are aware of something more.

However it is the first impact that is important in graphology; and to go beyond and to examine far deeper is something to be used at a later stage in this science. So this first moment is so important that it cannot be overemphasized, for as we establish the handwriting in what is known as its *form level*, (that is the group—or the grade—or position that it is to be placed in) we bring into play our sensory impression, our feeling. Our inner feeling touches the inner personality without knowing completely why we place one particular specimen in a higher position to another. So if we are given six specimens to look at we can say with practice—roughly—how they should go in *order of merit*—not based purely on beauty of outline, carefulness, fineness, but on something more. We are aware that logic and reason are not the only tools to use in this selection procedure, but a fine balance, based partly on intuition, partly on extrasensory perception in our

[handwriting sample]

6: Natural handwriting

Male. Aged 49. Executive. Director. Capable, confident, progressive, deals with pure essentials, generous, correct, balanced, slight reserve, intuitive and perceptive, gets ideas, optimistic, intelligent, broad outlook, slight inner depressions. Deals with personnel.

Group A

[handwriting sample]

7: Unnatural handwriting

Female. Aged 43. Designer. Original outlook. Does not conform to set pattern. Likes to be observed. Meticulous over small details. Can enlarge on small matters. Desire to control. Striving. Intuitive. Gets ideas. Deep concentration. More diplomatic than friendly. Cautious.

Group B

relationship with people. For instance, if we take a party of people, there are certain members who stand out; we call this *personality*. It is hard to define—perhaps the ugliest person in the room is the most attractive, the most vital, the most entertaining, whereas the most beautiful is the most boring. So with handwriting. For now we come to the factor of *rhythm* and harmonious balance, spacing, layout, how the handwriting attracts the eye, how our own sensitivity picks up the reflection of handwriting, how we are drawn more to one specimen than another. We are touching the whole time the vibration of the writer's inner personality, for handwriting is beautiful because it expresses something living—it is alive—it never dies. Handwriting hundreds of years old under a magnifying glass lives on.

What then is this rhythm, this feeling of knowing, what is this life force that can be felt as one holds the specimen in the hand and looks down on it, or holds it at a distance? It is as though handwriting is transmitting its force towards the person who is about to analyse it and to place it in what is known as its *form level*. This is a field where there are no rules to be strictly adhered to. Some people have tremendous powers of perception, just as they walk into a room and 'feel and sense an atmosphere', so they can use the same sensory system to grade handwriting. In this particular sphere practice makes perfect and it is remarkable how soon this sense comes into play.

It will be noted that specimens of handwriting already shown in this book have quoted a *group letter or letters*. This method of assessment by group is based on a formula developed over a considerable period of time to act as a measure or reference for the form level procedure. The following diagram will give some idea of how people (according to graphological ratings) are divided into various groupings. It has been found that some people do not fall completely into one distinct group as so many factors are involved which can alter what is known as a 'clear position', so therefore there is often a blending of groupings.

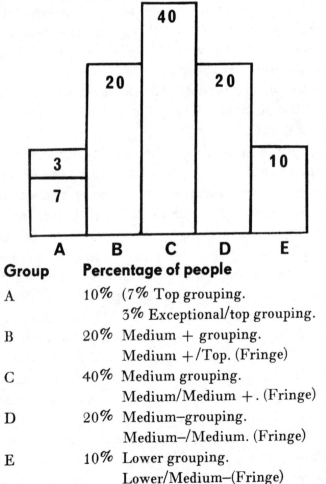

Group	Percentage of people
A	10% (7% Top grouping. 3% Exceptional/top grouping.
B	20% Medium + grouping. Medium +/Top. (Fringe)
C	40% Medium grouping. Medium/Medium +. (Fringe)
D	20% Medium−grouping. Medium−/Medium. (Fringe)
E	10% Lower grouping. Lower/Medium−(Fringe)

letter. I can't just lay my head or your lap are but as far as I remember your suggestions for the future boys are much in line with what they are doing.

8 (above): Form level positioning
Male. Aged 49. Executive. Director. Can take full responsibility. Goalminded. Logical. Analytical mind. Slight reserve. Directness of purpose. Active, alive, money motivated, very quick grasp of facts. Good vision and imagination, can observe over wide field of operations. Individualistic.
Group A (3%)

9 (below): Form level positioning

Male. Aged 43. Doctor. Advanced outlook particularly in psychiatric field. Leader type. Likes to control own sphere. Shows marked individualism. Sensitive. Highly flexible. Clear brain. Sociable. Inquiring and inquisitive mind. Intuitive. Likes movement and change. Shows slight inner depression. Can overwork.   Group A (7%)

Six specimens of handwriting are given under references (8) to (13). Examine these specimens carefully and say to yourself: 'would I also put these six specimens in this order'? If the answer is 'yes' then you have deduced the method being applied.

Take the top people. Then take the people you consider come into the medium + group and then those who come into the medium group. then those who come below into the medium – and lower groupings. One must first of all consider if the handwriting is natural or unnatural. There is a tendency today to copy some form of calligraphy, as per specimen (14). Such handwriting is usually outstandingly clear and brilliant, rather like a

10: Form level positioning
Female. Aged 25. Secretary. Positive. Active and ener-
getic. Firm, determined, likes to have own way.
Good judgment, can assess people. Realistic, practi-
cal. Secretive. Can deal with confidential work.
Dependable. Good organizer and co-ordinator.
Freshness and frankness. Slight reserve and restraint.
Caution. Enthusiastic. Slight vanity.
Group B

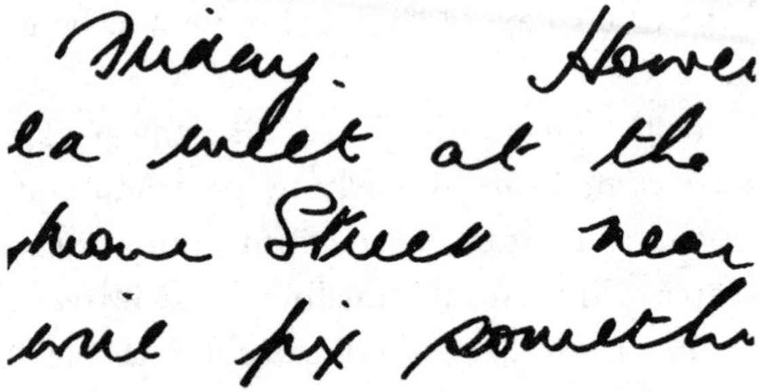

[handwritten cursive sample]

11: Form level positioning

Male. Aged 32. Salesman. Born sales type. Shows energy, vitality and willpower. Progressive. Not a born leader but likes to take control. Has bad temper submerged. Analytical and probing mind. Can be secretive. Likes to have own way. Could be difficult. Practical more than theoretical. Desire to achieve objective. Narrow background. A small matter can annoy and irritate.

Group C

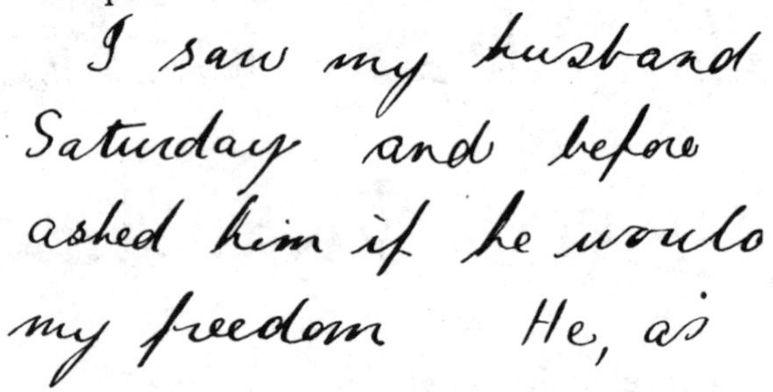

[handwritten cursive sample: "I saw my husband Saturday and before asked him if he would my freedom He, as"]

12: Form level positioning

Female. Aged 47. Narrow background. Knowledge limited. Sociable. Kind. Mood variations due to worry. Slight bad temper submerged. Clearminded. Non-complicated group. Lacks maturity for age grouping. Observant. Could exaggerate slightly. More diplomatic than friendly. Inner depression.

Group D

painting that is so meticulous that every brick is painted into the building. It is too good—too perfect—and although we are impressed, somehow we are not pleased. We say in the first instance that it is wonderful, but it offends the senses; we almost feel that the person who wrote this was vain, unnatural, trying to impress, introverted, trying to attract the reader, trying to induce into the reader's mind something that they would not forget. But this is a mask, an artificiality, and so we may put it aside and look for something more. Even in the case of apparently ugly handwriting we notice that at a distance it contains spirit, naturalness and liveliness, rather like an Impressionist painting by Renoir. On the surface it may lack essential detail; but if we observe the painting from a distance we see its beauty in its entirety.

All is rhythm. One senses intelligence—regularity, sureness—distribution of spaces in the handwriting. What we are looking for is the 'unknown

13: Form level positioning

Female. Aged 57. Not a strong or definite person. Lacks education. Highly money motivated. Not quite sure of herself. Very cautious. Marked reserve. Alternating moods. Lacks energy and resistance. Weakness of will. Calculating mind. Depressed.

Group E

ould like to say that writing to a
ologist is almost like
Father Confessor. — Hence the ha

14: Calligraphy

Male. Aged 38. Actor. Artistic. Sensitive. Intelligent. Careful. Well balanced, disciplined, deep concentration. Firm and determined. Good educational background. Meticulous to detail. Intuitive and perceptive. Very watchful. Directness. Frankness. Group B

quantity', as with people we meet on impact, we sense an intelligent person, we sense refinement, we sense knowledge, we sense leadership. Just as we sense the unintelligent, the coarse person, the person who pretends to be a leader, who puts on an 'act'—an adopted voice, a falseness. If we can detect defects in people so can we do this in handwriting. One looks for legibility but not for simplicity, one looks for speed, flow, movement, activity, boldness without flamboyance. One could almost say one looks for *sincere* handwriting and balanced handwriting, handwriting that indicates a high point of development.

For example a man scrawls a note to direct someone. It is free, uninhibited, alive, natural, it is free flowing, flexible: so even before the handwriting is read, the message is almost felt. The words make impact, they have meaning, but one *senses* the force behind the words. One senses how the subconscious mind has poured out its purpose, it has a sense of rhythm, so therefore rhythm, naturalness, spacing, symmetry, legibility and speed are all links in the chain that tells us, perhaps even subconsciously, that this particular specimen takes precedence over all other specimens; and we could use this as a marker and graduate all other specimens from this point. The less one brings in the purely analytical mind the better. The more one uses the sensory powers the more likely is one to achieve the main objective: that of establishing form level; and the importance of visualizing the writer's personality in its entirety before evaluation through the analytical principles of graphology.

The positioning of handwriting into its various zones

JUST as we have endeavoured in the previous chapter to segregate handwriting into form levels—top, medium and lower groups—so now we are going to place the individual specimens of handwriting into their various zones.

To explain this principle one can either visualize the whole of the twenty-six letters of the alphabet being written in scholastic style on lined foolscap similar to specimen (right) or better still to write the letters down yourself in order to get the 'feel' and meaning of this principle.

The zones are numbered (1) to (3)

(1) The upper zone.
(2) The middle zone.
(3) The lower zone.

It will be clearly observed that only the letters—

b   d   f   h   k   l   and   t

enter the upper zone. Also all capital letters.

It will be clearly observed that only the letters—

g   j   p   q   y   and   z

enter the lower zone.

There is only *one exception* and that is the letter f, which enters both upper and lower zones.

The rest of the alphabet consisting of the letters—

a   c   e   i   m   n   o   r   s   u   v   w   x

remain in the middle zone.

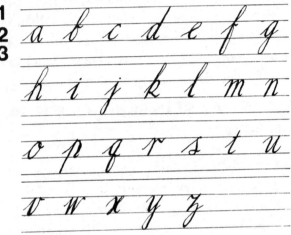

For the purpose of analysing handwriting we interpret the zones in the following manner:—

Zone (1) upper zone

This concerns the intellectual and spiritual spheres of development, and it can sometimes include also religious aspirations. This area can indicate the striving and idealistic qualities in an individual, the imagination and vision, the seeking of perfection. This zone can also be linked with the extension of the ego—the super-ego. In some cases the writer will extend the upper loop outside the zone completely; the handwriting will be so formed that the other two zones will appear to be insignificant and the full emphasis on the upper zone will be very clearly seen. The main thing is to realize that any *abnormality* in the formation of the upper loop, that is writing which is out of balance in comparison with the accepted style laid down, allows the analyst to accept that this subconscious development links itself with certain psychological processes outside the normal—tremendous striving for perfection, ideals, even into a world of fantasy outside realistic understanding. See specimen (16).

Zone (2) middle zone

Here is the balance—the overall balance—the pivot. This zone concerns reality, daily routine, the ego, consciousness of one's self in relation to others, materialism, self-centredness, social relationships. From this point everything stems. An over-emphasis of this zone indicates extreme realism wherever there is an encroachment into the upper zone. See specimen (17)

Zone (3) lower zone

Here we enter the analytical sphere. The sexual sphere. Deep materialistic impulses. Probing. Here

explaining my decision of Italy and Spain as be,

36

16: Upper zone loop formation

Male. Aged 21. Student/trainee industry. Restless. Sensitive. Seeks to start a new life as a singer. Has strong fantasy in the character structure also uncertainty as to way he is going. Intelligent within limited field. External good looks and voice. Can be very obstinate. Gets ideas. Strong individualism.

Group C

17 (below): Middle zone formation

Female. Aged 44. Very realistic and practical. Powerful personality. Strong-willed. Original although with considerable veneer. Likes to be different and puts on 'act'. Money motivated. Richness of inner resources. Capacity for organization. Domineering tendency. Tenacious. Obstinate. Ideas can germinate.

Group A/B

are the emotional links with sex. Self-Analysis. Instinct. Intuition. The subconscious. Thoughts below the surface.

A full explanation will be given later in another chapter on loops and their meanings; but it is necessary to establish the zone we are to operate in when commencing to analyse. We must ask the question: are we involved with a *major middle zone*, or is the emphasis on the *upper* zone or the *lower*? After practice one can assess quickly the type of person we are dealing with, whether *basically* idealistic and perfectionist, or normal and

Character traits (Upper Zone)

Positive qualities
Marked idealism and perfectionism
Spiritual aspirations
Desire to reach the unobtainable
Continual striving for perfection
Desire for independence of action
Desire for freedom of expression
Ambition towards an ideal
Intellectualism
Cultural aspirations
Variation in interests

Negative qualities
Remoteness from reality
Lacking of firm foundation
Lack of self-discipline
Could live in fantasy world
Forgetfulness
Difficult to understand or to make contact
Outside normal groupings

Character traits (Lower Zone)

Positive qualities
Strong materialistic trend
Organizer
Complete lack of any form of illusion
Deep probing and analytical mind
Self-analytical
Self-sufficient
Would take responsibility
Sexual influences. Must have outlet
Life must revolve on firm foundation
Belief only in realistic approach to everything

Negative qualities
Set pattern
Lack of understanding of others particularly those
    in the upper zone
Desire for sexual excitement
Could be sensual
Lacks the ability to adjust
Pretentiousness

Character traits (Middle Zone)

Positive qualities

Practical	Factual
Realistic	Well balanced outlook
Firmness	Not easily moved
Determination	Strong willed

Negative qualities

Desire to dominate	Self-opinionated
Desire to have own way	Would not accept criticism
Awareness of the immediate	One track mind
Strong ego force	Could lack essential vision

realistic, or someone who is highly analytical and who lives in a very firmly rooted materialistic and positive world. If the handwriting is well balanced throughout all three zones, we are very much within the normal sphere—without extremes. Whilst it is necessary to discuss the zonal area it will be seen later that there are many facets that can alter the whole picture of the graphological analysis.

Zoning is interesting: just as we would refer to a person being 'very idealistic' or 'very materialistic' or 'very deep', so we assess by placing handwriting into zones.

Outstanding graphological signs to look for

1. Size

THERE are various ways of assessing the size of handwriting. One can measure and establish a formula. For example one may use $\frac{1}{8}$th inch (or 3 mm) as 'normal' for the small letters. This would be within the middle zone category. Anything above the $\frac{1}{8}$th inch (or 3 mm) would be considered larger than normal. One method is to measure lines on to a form of tracing paper allowing a space of $\frac{1}{8}$th inch (3 mm), in order that the measurement area can be placed over the handwriting in question, so that it can be seen through the tracing paper and the size ascertained. Many people use this method with every piece of handwriting they analyse; but it is considered that to gauge and assess handwriting into size categories *at a glance* is the best method. The size of handwriting is grouped as large, medium and small. One is immediately aware of exceptionally large handwriting as per specimen (18) this applies also to signatures. Much can be learned from the size of handwriting.

Large

Just as a tall man can stand out in a crowd and be observed, so with handwriting. One observes large handwriting, in fact the larger it becomes the more easily it is noticed. The writer reflects strongly his subconscious feelings. His need for space. His feeling of self-importance. To be observed. To be bold. To accept a challenge. To impress at times. To win recognition. One almost senses the 'type' of man or woman who writes large handwriting. They can often be small in stature; but handwriting is not associated with physical characteristics. One could assume that a very large person could at times write a large hand; but it would be highly dangerous to 'imagine' the size of a person by his or her handwriting, just as to imagine age. Any such assessment or guess would prove with time unreliable. The positive and negative qualities closely associated with large handwriting are as follows:—

Character traits (Large)

Positive qualities		*Negative qualities*
Self-reliance	Independence	Haughtiness
Seriousness	Organizing ability	Boastfulness
Superiority	Pride	Desire to impress
Generosity	Expansive outlook	Lack of discipline
Optimism	Boldness	Lack of care

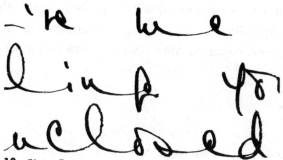

18: Size — Large

Female. Aged 41. Bold. Determined. Very marked
judgment. Firm. Would accept a challenge. Realistic
and practical. Alive. Energetic. Enthusiastic. Vision
and foresight. Accurate. Sociable. Warmth. Need
for praise and encouragement. Slight vanity and
conceit. Constructive and logical. Intelligent. Ideas
germinate.

Group A

19: Size — Small

Male. Aged 61. Highly intelligent. Academic mind.
Careful. Concentrated type of brain. Logical.
Adaptable. Accurate. Works very hard. Slight exhaustion and depression indicated. Leader type.
Flexible. Individualist. Quick grasp of facts. Good
vision and foresight. Imagination. Comes to the
point quickly.

Group A

Medium and normal balanced handwriting invariably belongs to a person who is neither overestimating or underestimating himself with others, they usually like to conform to normal standards. We now come to small size handwriting as per specimen (19).

Small

Just as a small man feels that he could be overlooked in a crowd, and can envy the tall man who is observed automatically, so he has compensations in the handwriting field. Very small handwriting can indicate a high degree of concentration, realism, sometimes intentional understatement, a distaste for boasting; it can also link up with an inferiority complex, modesty, executive ability and academic mentality. In fact in general the man who writes small handwriting is more inclined to channel his energies into thinking rather than action.

The positive and negative qualities closely associated with small handwriting are as follows:—

Character traits (Small)

Positive qualities
Concentration
Conscientiousness
Accuracy
Modesty
Tolerance
Adaptability
Scrutiny
Executive ability
Individuality
Specialization
Critical mindedness
Reserve
Power to assimilate
Theoretical mind
Business acumen
Studious
Thoughtful
Strong inclination for detail

Negative qualities
Pettiness
Fear
Submissiveness
Can be an inability to see
things in larger aspect
Lack of self-confidence
Over-scrupulousness
Economical mind
Lack of enthusiasm
Fussiness
Pedantry
Can get despondent

2. Slant

WHEN we refer to slant in handwriting we mean that the downward or upward strokes tilt away from the vertical, this swing either to the left or the right should be within an area of 45° from the vertical. If it exceeds 45° then we enter what is known as the extreme group of slant. Handwriting is considered upright within a 5° area either way. One must visualize handwriting standing on a base line as per diagram showing slant fluctuation.

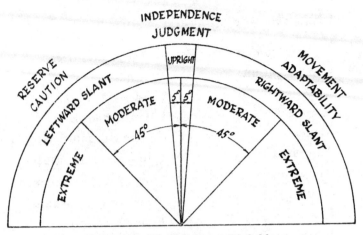

SLANT FLUCTUATION

The various methods of teaching throughout the world would indicate that there is a considerable emphasis towards the rightward slant, but due to so-called 'new methods' of teaching handwriting, for clarity reasons, one finds forms of printed letters in an upright position which is a form of enforced handwriting, but despite all the various *methods* of teaching one fact remains: that there are never in the end two handwritings exactly alike.

If a person has been taught to write with a rightward slant at school to conform with a set method of teaching, there can occur with considerable frequency, a tendency for them either to write upright or even to commence writing backwards at a later date in life. In fact the slant position must be always considered as the *desire* of the writer. So if at school the pattern taught was the rightward slant and in consequence the writer feels subconsciously that this suits his own inner sense he will continue to write in this direction. Likewise if a person is taught to write upright and they feel subconsciously the tendency to write upright they will also continue with this pattern. But due to *individualism* any training which is essentially the transference of another person's thought or idea, either through the scholastic profession or a calligraphic organization, will never obliterate the normal tendency of the writer to write *exactly as he or she feels.* Therefore we must view the slant position (particularly in adult handwriting) as an indication of personality and desire. An *inner feeling* to write in one particular way.

In examining children's handwriting after leaving school, one notes sometimes remarkable and immediate changes. (Parents would do well to note the handwriting of their children over a considerable period both at school and on entry into adult life, by keeping specimens at monthly intervals.) If the study of graphology is maintained so much can be learned from children's handwriting that parents may find themselves in a position to help as they would never have been able to do otherwise.

In accepting that the method of teaching has originally established the slant or angle of the handwriting, and also accepting that everyone will write as they *feel*, and that no two handwritings are ever completely alike, we will now generalize on the overall meaning of the various slants, commencing with the rightward slant as specimen (20).

Character traits (Rightward)

Positive qualities
Adaptability
Sociability
Dexterity
Social ease

Sociability
Activity
Initiative
Spontaneousness
Enthusiasm

More activity than contemplation
Communicativeness
Optimism
Self-sacrifice
Sense of enterprise
Empathy
Unselfishness
Humanitarianism
Desire to give
Expressiveness
Devotion
Affection

Negative qualities

Lack of restraint
Lack of control
Impatience
Haste
Restlessness
Sometimes lack of discipline
Thoughtlessness
Irritability
Distractability
Easily influenced
Lack of good judgment
Desire to have own way
Immoderateness
Sometimes blindness for danger
Fickleness
Verbosity
Over-adaptibility
Happy go lucky outlook
Morbidness
Dependence on others
Violence can occur at times

Rightward slant

The person who normally uses the rightward slant within the range of 45° belongs to the sociable group, where human relationships are important. They sometimes belong to the full extravert group; and they are usually active and goal-minded. They seek recognition and the regard of others; and they can be enthusiastic and continually looking into the future. They can be restless and need variety and change. If the handwriting goes over the 45° and enters the extreme group, one finds strong emotional trends developing: love, passion, hate and also self-sacrifice. This can also link with an excitable temperament with uncontrolled behaviour. Briefly the rightward slant is the link with the outside world away from self and towards others.

20: Rightward slant

Male. Aged 37. Nigerian. Outstanding brain. Vision, foresight and imagination. Strong creativeness. Positive and strong. Endurance. Energy, vitality and willpower. Impatient. Deep concentration. Individualist. Intuitive and perceptive. Ideas germinate. Can organize and co-ordinate. Leader type. Understands European mind.

Group A

Leftward slant

Here is the complete opposite of the rightward slant. It will be observed that there are far fewer people who use this type of handwriting. This is the minority group. One will also find more women than men using this type of slant therefore a woman's handwriting has been chosen as an example in this case as per specimen (21)

The writer, quite apart from any external sociability, is nevertheless very much more reserved and withdrawn from the world at large and only comes out to join in when necessary. There can be a form of inner isolation, repression, an interest in people in a detached way, a form of abstraction. There is always some form of barrier between the writer and the outside world: the cautionary factor and reserve act like a brake on any spontaneous reaction, and there can be a form of self-consciousness and even timidity. They can be very sensitive. It would seem that left-handed writers would automatically write backwards; but this is not always the case and should be noted when examining a person writing with a left hand. Just as the rightward slant produces emotional trends so the leftward slant can cause unemotional and cold trends. There is more self-interest in this group and usually there can be traced strong family links either from the mother or father, a form of over protection and love. They can have strong ties within the whole family area and seldom free their memories from past environmental experiences.

Character traits (Leftward)

Positive qualities

Introspection

Control

Reserve

Self-conquest

Precaution

Holding back

Freedom from illusions

Sense of self-account

Independence

Determination

Accentuation on memory

Self-collection

Ambition

Sometimes fear of future

Abstraction

Self-loyalty

Sense of self-preservation

Reflexiveness

Caution

Meditativeness

Negative qualities

Artificiality

Affectation

Forced behaviour

Self-consciousness

Conceit

Arrogance

Absence of deep emotion

Cynicism

Unapproachable

Pretentiousness

Selfishness

Over-sensitivity

Resentment

Cruelty

Envy

Egotism

Desire to take

Narcissism

Jealousy

21 : Leftward slant

Female. Aged 36. Canadian. Active. Intelligent. Leader. Strong desire to control. Good organizer and co-ordinator. Secretive. Could enlarge on small matters. Enthusiastic. Realistic and practical. Need for praise and encouragement. Slight vanity and conceit. Critical. Sceptical. Can assess people. Reserved. Very watchful. Senses a situation. Very down to earth. Reliable.

Group A

22 : Upright slant

Female. Aged 43. Business executive. Independent. Flexible and adaptable. Slight reserve. Marked introversion. Leader type. Concentration. Impatient. Quick grasp of facts. Sceptical. Selective. Sincerity. Kindness. Objective. Individualist. Small matters are important. Must work with people she is in harmony with to produce best results. Desire for freedom of action.

Group B

Upright slant

This is the middle course. The independent group who are less dependent on outside influences. The completely upright hand is rare, but the variations within the 5° area are accepted as per specimen (22).

Usually the writer displays calmness and judgment, poise, realism, and can meet problems in a calm manner. He or she will show reasons rather than emotion, and any form of impulse can be corrected by this fine balance. In the case of children, one finds they are more inclined to rely on themselves and make their own way through life independently of the parents, and like to be recognized by the parents for their independence of manner and outlook.

The positive and negative qualities closely associated with upright slant handwriting are as follows:—

Character traits (Upright)

Positive qualities	*Negative qualities*
Self-collection	Indifference
Imperviousness	Egotism
Foresight	Self-containment
Sense of independence	Rigidity
Pride	Shut-offness
Unswerving attitude	Pessimism
Weighing up of words	Coldness
Scepticism	Lack of external interest
Personal distance	Lack of empathy
Control and restraint	Snobbishness
Coolheadedness	Unresponsiveness
Self-command	Seclusion

Reliability	Detachment
Can work well on own	Lack of sentimentality
Impartiality	Lack of emotion
Calmness	Reticence
Poise	Inhibition
Realistic	Resignation

Variations: mixed slant

In dealing with the three main slant groups we are bound to have variations. These include the extreme slant and the alternating slant as per specimen (23)

This is where a person will sometimes write upright, then slope backwards and then suddenly go forward towards the right. Such cases are fortunately rare and are largely connected with people who display subconscious uncertainty; or where there could be a conflict of an emotional nature; a form of inner struggle with resultant indecision and inconsistency. Sometimes the writer who varies his slants continually can be fighting strong emotional forces which are trying to override the brain force or vice versa. In such cases, once it has been established what the writer desires from life and where both emotional and mental forces have been brought together, the handwriting will then take on a more stabilized form. Any form of mood variation caused by atmosphere and environment can cause alteration in slant.

The positive and negative qualities closely associated with the mixed slant handwriting are as follows.

Character traits (Mixed)

Positive qualities	*Negative qualities*
Impressionability	Unstable
Agitation	Unpredictable
Nobility of feeling	Anxiety
Liveliness	Neurosis
Many interests	Depression
Versatility	Changeability
Desire for change and variety	Indecision
Creative genius	Moodiness
Mercurial	Inconsistency

23: Mixed slant

Female. Aged 42. Erratic. Nervous. Self-analytical. Has had considerable trouble. Uncertain. Lacks overall maturity and balance. Very diplomatic. Protective to family. Advanced mood variations due to atmosphere and environment. Need for security. Strong links with past. Uses calculation and strategy.

Group D

3. Spacing

Lines

WE now enter the field of organization and co-ordination. The clear and mature thinker invariably spaces the lines at equal distance from each other. The careful and conscientious person may have narrow spacing between lines but he still allows no letter from the previous line to overlap the other. There is no confusion. No mixing or crossing of under-lengths and upper-lengths. The distribution, although not consciously planned, measured or devised, presents to the graphologist the state of mind of the writer: whether it is orderly, whether the structure pattern is firmly constructive or erratic. Again we come back to the rhythmic content: does it present to the eye a balanced rhythmic quality? Specimens (24) and (25) are given to illustrate this point.

The writer has a plain piece of paper and he is going to communicate his thoughts. If he is clear and firm he will automatically space his lines at equal distance either wide or narrow in width.

Sensitive writers are usually aware of the artistic forming of the overall pattern and are therefore conscious of spacing. Often spacing between lines can vary according to mood, but the main thing to look for is clarity of spacing where one line is separate from the other. When the actual area of writing space is more than sufficient it is easy to separate the lines; but when the area is limited the clear-minded person will still allow for balanced spacing between lines even if it means reducing the size of his normal handwriting. Good spacing represents orderliness, clear thinking, surveying qualities and the power to elucidate.

Very wide spacing can indicate a certain detachment from others and a form of reserve as per specimen (26) (Page 58). whereas a narrow spacing can link with spontaneous reaction and lack of reserve. The middle course where spacing is very well balanced can be linked with a born organizer, the executive type; to the scholastic and university professions etc., especially where the power of thinking in the abstract is needed. When handwriting is either large, medium or small and starts to blend or interweave with the previous line we are aware of confusionary elements and lack of clarity.

Words

Every writer spaces his words without thought of the distance between words. The subconscious reaction in regard to spacing reflects the natural flow of recording thought impulses, just as when speaking there is the easy steady flow, or the hesitant flow. So with handwriting. Words follow one another either quickly or slowly: the writer can pause between each word and perhaps produce a fairly wide space, or he can write with great rapidity and still produce a wide space, or he can produce a narrow space.

It is essential to watch for the spaces between words, just as we watch for spaces between lines. A wide space can indicate a considerable degree of reserve and caution, thoughtfulness and sometimes shyness. However if the space is narrow we find the writer shows action, lacks reserve, and could become impatient. Such writers are inclined to be 'self-contained units' generating immediate power and action. They can be very self-confident.

*I very much hope that in-
volve some modus operandi.
. If it can be arranged,
two can make an invaluable
in side of personal assess-
say, we had best keep this
for now.*

24: Spacing. Lines Clear
Male. Aged 47. Personnel officer and Director. Deals
with pure essentials. Meticulous. Sensitive. Very
well balanced and intelligent. Clearminded. Academic. Modest. Intuitive. Ideas can germinate.
Slight reserve. Very correct. Accurate. Keen assessment of others. Sociable. Concentration. Conscientiousness. Scrutiny of observation. Theoretical class.
Executive ability.
Group A

Again we must look for the rhythmic balance.
The spacing must be regular—either wide or narrow.
This is the key note in making the analysis; and
when we find alternating spaces we must accept
that there are periods of reserve and caution and
even calculation.

As one's own private dossier is built up from
known cases the question of spacing will become
more and more important and take on a very definite meaning, and will act as a very positive
guide.

57

25 (above): Spacing Lines Mixed

Female. Aged 51. Active. Restless. Has had considerable
bad health. Atmosphere and environment most
important. Can get irritated. Confused by situations.
Worried. Analyses and probes everything. Gets
depressed. Very inquiring and inquisitive mind.
Small matters can be enlarged—Secretive.

Group C

26 (below): Wide spacing
Male. Aged 29. Opera singer. Sensitive. Susceptibl
to atmosphere and environment. Reserve and
restraint. Marked judgment. Observant. Deep concentration. Sociable. Constructive outlook. Slight
isolation and loneliness. Feminine trend. Very inquiring and inquisitive mind. Planning and surveying ability.

Group B

Margins

Margins can be likened to a frame surrounding a picture: in this case the picture is composed of handwriting. We can have a broad margin completely round the picture, or we can have a narrow one. We can have a broad left margin with a narrow right margin, we can have two narrow margins with a broad margin at the top (sometimes caused by the letter heading) but with a broad margin at the base. In fact we can have quite a variety of margins but all have a meaning graphologically.

The left hand margin is selected by ourselves. We all start to write at a certain point. We establish a marker—this being the first word—either on the first or second line dependent on any indenture on the first line. This marker establishes whether by choice we prefer a wide or a narrow margin; but again our subconscious mind plays its part in the form of selection.

From the marker the writing moves towards the right until it reaches a point conditioned either by a word termination or on impulse to return to the next line. Again the subconscious mind is establishing a margin formation to be either narrow, wide or irregular.

Left hand margin

A wide left margin can in many cases establish a good cultural background. This can link with heredity; it can also indicate a consciousness of one's own values and a form of pride and refinement. It can also indicate generosity, reserve, and even a form of snobbishness.

A narrow left hand margin can indicate a limited

family background, a sense of economy, informality, and sometimes a desire for popularity. It can indicate a desire to build up a secure life and to release oneself from a narrow field. It is interesting to note how through the heredity link this margin is carried on to successive generations, even though money and education have obliterated the limited background.

If either type of margin continues to widen towards the bottom of the page, this can indicate an inner tiredness and even at times exhaustion, caused by such factors as haste, impatience and enthusiasm. Likewise if the margin tends to narrow, this can indicate a conservation of strength and a control over the outflow of energy, cautiousness, prudence and reduced spontaneity. Just as the left hand margin is *controlled* and *established* and is maintained throughout, the right hand margin is forming itself and in this field one can analyse the writer's relationship with others.

Right hand margin

Should the right margin be formed broadly, almost in width equal to the left, then the reserve in the character is enhanced. There can be feelings of fear as to the future and oversensitivity; also an inability to face up completely to reality. Feelings of self-consciousness are also often present.

Should the margin form itself into a narrow formation almost bringing the words to the edge of the paper, there is shown courage in facing up to life and problems, communicativeness, haste, vitality and a lack of inhibitions. There could also be some link with suspicion and scepticism.

Wide upper margin

When a writer surveys the sheet of writing paper and his subconscious mind visualizes the addressee, he will express in his handwriting his degree of esteem. Should the paper be embossed with the address he will naturally start with the date; but should there be no address and if he commences by leaving a wide margin he will emphasise his respectfulness, formality, and general modesty.

Narrow upper margin

Likewise when he leaves a very narrow upper margin, there is indicated his degree of informality, directness of approach, lack of respect and form of indifference. Also an inability to see and appreciate the varying degrees of human achievement.

Wide lower margin

In viewing the lower margin we are faced with the termination of a letter or document. This may produce a wide lower margin, but should the writer wish to produce a wide lower margin through his subconscious mind as is often the case, this can indicate superficiality, aloofness, idealism, reserve and aesthetic sense.

Narrow lower margin

As the writer commences to use the sheet of writing paper he visualizes how he can fill or partially fill it with words. Some writers instinctively like to use only a few words whereas others use as many as possible; and in this latter group we find the writer who usually uses the narrow lower margin. He is by nature a communicative individual, realistic and materialistic, he can also belong, strange as it may seem, to the sentimental and dreamer groups; and he can also suffer from depressions.

Margins of equal width all round

This group is rare. It means that the writer has both a *consciousness* of left and right margins, also upper and lower. They belong to a world where atmosphere and environment and colour are vital. There can be a form of reserve and isolation, a philosophical and spiritual independence, and a secrecy about their affairs. They desire to impress others by their appearance and they can have strong artistic and aesthetic sensibilities. They have a liking for neatness and orderliness, and are concerned with details. They can be very withdrawn.

All margins missing

Here is another rare group. Here the writer cuts out all barriers between himself and others. This group can cause very strong positive and negative reactions. Intrusion or sympathy, kindness or tactlessness, generosity or greed, sincere interest or idle curiosity. There can also be lack of taste or any form of refinement, and little concern for propriety or for other people's privacy.

It will be observed that much can be learned from margins. A very careful study is advised from specimens of known handwriting contained in the private dossier, and from these specimens further information can be added to that already provided in this book, the latter endeavours to give the outstanding facets in the character structure.

4. Direction of lines

AGAIN we must revert to our early formative days at school where we were instructed on lined note-paper. It was a long time before we were ever allowed to use unlined paper unless it was for private letters; and therefore it would be fair to say that the percentage of writing was mainly carried out on lined paper. This gave us direction. We had a feeling of a basic line. A guide. As long as we could keep on this line all was well. We never noticed if our writing was alternating, whether it sometimes slipped just below the line, or whether it was well above the line. These lines were to enable us to write straight and level, yet with all the tuition hardly anyone ever did or could continue for any length of time completely straight and level handwriting. If we examine words closely we will note alternations, waves in the words, up and down motions: that is movement *within* words, not only within whole sentences; even though the sentences themselves show considerable variations.

We have dealt with spaces between words and between lines; now we are going to deal with the lines themselves. Here perhaps is one of the most powerful of all reflections connected with graphic movement. We are able at a glance to observe whether the overall picture presents handwriting which is either—

(a) Near level.

(b) Ascending.

(c) Descending.

Whether it is calm and uniform, or whether it is erratic and lacks the essential rhythmic quality. At a glance from a position of about three feet, all is very clear. We can group handwriting into one of *little frightening.*

As a newly fledged teacher I shall be particularly interested in the development of young people's handwriting in relation to the development of their personalities. No doubt you and I will perhaps be able to share our interests in this respect and compare notes.

In the meantime please accept my very best wishes for your venture and may we hear a lot more of you in the future.

Yours sincerely,

Kenneth

27: Near level

Male. Aged 40. Schoolmaster. Here one notes the clear progressive and level handwriting of the writer. Clear margin, well balanced and planned formation of letter, in itself a 'word picture'. The writer has become a schoolmaster after having made a change in his career at a late date. He is neither over-optimistic or depressed by the new experience; one almost senses with the handwriting the keen approach to a new task and the clarity of outlook. As no handwriting is exactly level one must note the variations in the words with slight downward trends, but the overall impression is one of levelness.

Group B

in this situation I think I'm afraid of
being a disappointment (after successful
"Mothers") — and yet when everything was
truly right & I loved, I have asked my
mind comes into so, before during & after
& that's why everything must be
right — to prevent my mind from
working. So I guess I accepted this
too, along with other things are discussed
yesterday, I can be neither
        The dilemma is the same, it just dawned
on me, as it must have been years ago —
does he — my father — want me to fulfil will
This is what I think I am still thinking
about anyone interested in me. If he does,
then I have a tendency to be unnatural
or babyish. But the big thing I think is
that this dilemma is going on in my mind all
the time when I am alone with a man

28: Ascending

Female. Aged 29. Sales Manageress. The ascending
lines of the handwriting is very clear in this case,
perhaps slightly above normal, but this is a case
where the writer is putting down on paper some of
her innermost thoughts, she is pouring out from
the subconscious mind many things that have
puzzled her in her life; the fact that she has the
opportunity to do this and to get rid of so much to
someone prepared to read about her problem has
given her tremendous pleasure and therefore her
handwriting clearly indicates the inner emotional
force.

Group B

the three groups—

(a) Balanced.

(b) Optimistic.

(c) Depressive.

These groups are naturally based on a broad out-line. The direction of the handwriting from left

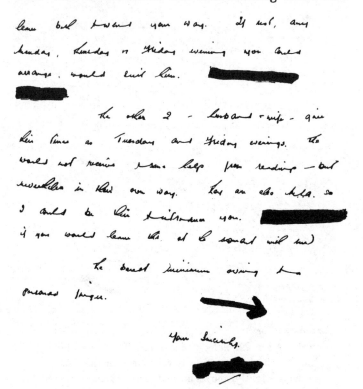

29: Descending

Female. Aged 57. This is a person of independent means, who although travelling continually throughout the world never finds true happiness. Suffers from acute loneliness and depression. Very introverted, reserved, modest and cautious. Has good family background, is always seeking something new to act as a stimulus. Has moods, is very secretive. Likes to be different from others.   Group B to right can be interpreted as time motion; for each letter can represent past, present and future in its movement towards the right. It is a form of constructive motion built up in words, each one to be carefully examined in regard to the positioning of the individual letters forming the word in question. In this way a line of handwriting consists of letters, words and sentences moving towards an ultimate objective. This objective can take many forms. But there is a goal. It could be a letter of congratulation, a letter of condolence, a business letter, a love letter. It could be a report, a statement, an outline of a planned project, in fact it can be anything. But whatever the objective is in writing the subconscious mind reflects mood variations, that are part of the deep subconscious mind which functions right outside the factual side of man and portrays those elements known as optimism, enthusiasm, zeal, depression, fatigue, unhappiness, worry etc., in fact it mirrors the whole range of emotions. For the purpose of explanation three case histories are given for observation. (See specimens (27) (28) and (29).

5. Speed

WE are all aware of the speed with which we write. Almost at once, if questioned, we can say with certainty, that we write either quickly or slowly. We know if pressed that we can write exceptionally quickly, or that if we are elated the tendency is to increase the speed. We could almost indicate if necessary our minimum and maximum speeds. Often other people observe our movements, our naturalness of expression, our self-assurance, our agility, our overall liveliness, vitality and energy. Likewise they would observe our slowness, our thoughtfulness and our steadiness in everything we do. As a result, observation of movement allows others to assess us in regard to quickness and slowness in handwriting. But they are not really concerned in such an assessment; however if they were called upon to pass judgment it is felt that they would be reasonably accurate. When reviewing handwriting we are aware of the activity it displays on *impact* and we call this speed. It is a vital part in the complete graphological assessment.

To assess *quickness* we have many guides to help us. They are as follows:—

(1) Observance of 'i' dots and 't' crossings.
(When they are to the *right side* of the stem)

(2) When 'i' dots look like dashes.

(3) Fluency. Unbroken strokes.

(4) Rightward slant.

(5) Ascending lines.

(6) Connected handwriting.

(7) Wide script.

(8) No adjustments. Free flowing. Smoothness.

(9) Sometimes an increasing left margin.

(10) Lively endings to finishing strokes and words.

(11) No change in direction.

To assess *slowness* the following are useful guides:—

(1) Observance of 'i' dots and 't' crossings.
(When they are either straight over, or to the *left side* of the stem)

(2) Leftward slant, or left tendency on movement.

(3) Noticeably artificial handwriting showing marked carefulness. Ornamentation.

(4) Descending lines.

(5) Narrow formation of handwriting.

(6) Slow initial strokes.

(7) Any alterations in direction of flow.

(8) Alterations in words.

The above are but a few of the indications which can be seen and clearly felt on impact.

31 (above): Speed. Quick

Female. Aged 58. Executive/Press. Drive. Energy. Vision. Goalminded. Imagination. Can co-ordinate. Clear thinking. Zeal. Purposefulness. Logic. Constructive outlook. Fluent thought. Impulse. Friendliness and diplomacy combined. Sincere. Need for praise and encouragement. Foresight.   Group A

30 (below): Speed. Quick

Male. Aged 39. Executive/Consultant. Industry. Alive. Alert. Flexible. Impatient. Progressive. Logical. Very quick grasp of facts. Vivacious. Clearminded. Intelligent. Practical and realistic approach. Leadership. Desire for freedom of action. Very goalminded. Could be secretive.   Group A

A few minutes to spare. Could we please speak about this?

Character traits (Quick)

Positive qualities

Quickness in thinking
Objectiveness
Direction towards target
Need for change
Need for stimulation
Vivacity
Intelligence
Zeal
Agility
Interest. Initiative

Energy and vitality
Impulse
Temperament
Mental activity
Self-assurance
Naturalness of expression
Foresight
Ambition
Spontaneity
Elasticity
Goalmindedness
Could adjust rapidly
   to new situations
Desire for variety

Negative qualities

Could lack analytical approach
Absentmindedness
Superficial manner
Lack of planning ability
Lack of steadiness
Excitable

Could be influenced
Rashness
Aimlessness
Could lack concentration
Lack of reliability
Lack of definite thinking

Below is an example of slow handwriting, specimen
(32), and the positive and negative qualities which
can be associated with such writing.

me when I was staying at Runton,
at deal about archaeology. I would
.teful if you could be of any help, as
at not having heard anything for suc
ried several other sources to gain infor

32: Speed. Slow

Male. Aged 20. Student. Archaeology. Reserved. Sensitive. Steadiness. Caution. Carefulness. Deals with essentials. Neatness. Contemplativeness. Thoughtfulness. Accuracy. Individualistic. Non-leader type. Preciseness.   Group C/D

Character traits (Slow)

Positive qualities	*Negative qualities*
Steadiness	Passivity
Contemplativeness	Hesitancy
Carefulness	Cautiousness
Thrift	Inactivity
Self-control	Inner tension
Balance	Irresponsibility
Considerateness	Anxiety moods
Preciseness	Depression
Prudence	(Watch also for downward tren
Neatness	Unsteadiness
Caution	Inflexibility
Consistency	Carelessness
Coolheadedness	Indolence
Calmness	Lack of energy
Sometimes introversion	Indecisiveness
Economy	Weak will
Thoroughness	Gullibility

6. Pressure

The use of pen or ball point pen

WHEN we choose a pen we reflect our personality. Today with the ubiquitous use of the fountain pen and the individual's command over an almost continuous flow of ink, the choice of the nib is of paramount importance: also the fact, that we subconsciously consider a pen to be a very personal acquisition and possibly a life-long possession, is of importance. Firms who deal in the sale of pens can assess on impact (that is on external appearance) the possible type of pen to be chosen by a customer.

In carrying out preliminary tests of nibs we engage in what is known as primary and secondary pressures. The primary pressure is the first instance where the pen touches the paper (that is the first resistance of the paper surface according to its texture). One senses this resistance. Test paper is usually slightly glazed to allow the writer to feel as little resistance as possible. This pressure is of course invisible but sensed. On the commencement of writing in the normal way, what is known as secondary pressure comes into play. This is the pressure normally used in handwriting. The pen is gripped, either firmly or lightly, and the graphic motion begins across the paper, producing heavy, medium or light pressure.

In the case of the ball point pen the level of assessment between primary and secondary pressures is lowered, as the result is universal by the nature of the structure of the pen.

To ascertain the varying pressures (of handwriting) the graphologist must use his magnifying glass. The surface movement of the ball point will establish pressure and will also indent the paper on the reserve side. This can also confirm heavy or low pressure. Before commencing to study pressures it is a good idea to practice with various types of pens and ball point pens to see results. These results can be included in the dossier with any remarks considered necessary. Under magnification the ball point pen reflects pressure in a very different way from the ordinary pen, as will be observed in practice. But as the ball point pen is used increasingly more nowadays, the ascertainment of pressure reflections must be carefully observed as a separate issue of study.

For the purpose of graphological assessment pressures have been divided into two distinctly clear groups, heavy, see specimen (33) and light, see specimen (34)- and the positive and negative qualities associated with these groups are given below:—

Character traits (Heavy)

Positive qualities
Energy, vitality
Tenacity
Conscientiousness
Willpower
Conscientiousness with marked endurance
Determination
Steadiness towards objective
Self-control
Ability to take decisions
Controlled impulse
Would accept a challenge
Fearlessness

A blurred, heavy impression — personal enough to be swirled around like cigarette in a class. Insideout

feel into focus, because excel + insight, the much dear

details in reflected light — and fade. Much more contain

to remember by ink — Dear Diary, today I saw her

standing in the line for the ski tow, weather, clothes

33 (above): Pressure. Heavy
Male. Aged 27. Independent. Firm. Obstinate. Very
secretive. Can exaggerate his own importance. Likes
to have own way and be in limelight. Involved within himself. Deep concentration. Realistic and practical. Stubbornness. Inhibitions. Down to earth.
 Little illusion.
Group C/D

76

34 (below): Pressure. Light

Female. Aged 22. German origin. Secretary. Sensitive.
Impressionable. Flexible. Adaptable. Tolerance.
Receptiveness. Friendliness and diplomacy. Kind.
Secretive. Can adjust herself to new situations. Re-
alistic. Good organizer. Introverted. Inquiring mind.
Need for praise and encouragement. Slight vanity.

Group C

Are you still frozen up ? Today it is
trouble and grey here. Yesterday I wa
and today I am in a mixed mood.
because I have to keep my appointmen
A German friend (50-50) has come
has for three weeks and wants to see u

Negative qualities

Vanity and conceit (look for confirmation with
    letters 't' and 'd'

Stubborness

Could be obstinate

Impulsiveness

Desire to have own way without due thought of
    consequence

Irritability

Could be difficult to understand

Aggressiveness

Character traits (Light)

Positive qualities	*Negative qualities*
Sensitivity	Timidity
Sometimes femininity	Could lack determination
Can be very adaptable	Could lack initiative
Flexible	Could yield under pressure
Adjustable to new situations	Lack of energy
Mobility	Weak willed
General overall awareness	Lack of inner resistance
Tolerance	Lack of endurance
Sympathetic understanding	Forcelessness
Receptiveness	Unreliable
Modesty	Lack of steadiness
Alertness	Superficial
Expediency	Irritability
Agility	Touchiness
Susceptible to atmosphere	Could be easily offended

As explained in the chapter on form level there
can be no completely distinct group and there must
be some form of blending with pressures as
follows:—

Medium heavy pressure

In this group one finds the majority of people coming from all walks of life, although this group can reflect at times both heavy and light pressures according to mood variations, such as anger, frustration and high dregrees of sensitivity caused by atmosphere and environment. The main thing is to assess by magnification whether the writer is tending more towards one pressure or the other.

Extreme light pressure

Such handwriting can indicate lack of vitality, energy and goalmindedness. This so-called pressureless handwriting must be carefully analysed in conjunction with all other factors before giving a final assessment. Look also for signs of depression.

7. Shading of writing

Pasty and sharp script

IN dealing with the pressure applied to the pen and the various results obtained from heavy, medium and light pressures we now enter the field where handwriting is to be assessed on whether or not it is distinct or sharp, or whether it is indistinct and has the appearance of pastiness. Pasty script is assessed by observing the up and down strokes as being of equal thickness, almost as if the writing was painted or a thick nib had been deliberately used. Whereas sharp script as the name applies has the reverse tendency; here there is a very marked difference in the up and down strokes. The *shading* of the writing, although linked naturally with *pressure*, can often occur where hardly

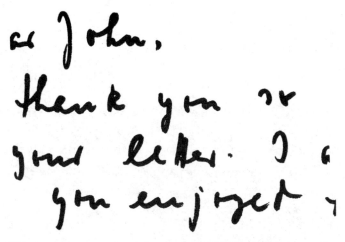

35: Shading of handwriting. Pasty. Pressureless

Female. Aged 38. Independent. Highly intuitive. Shows
warmth. Impressionability. Readiness to accept
new situations. Desire for good living. Constructive.
Good organizer. Deep concentration. Intensity of
reality experience. Logical. Intelligent. Ideas can
germinate. Accurate. Wide scope of available experience. Small matters can annoy.   Group B

any pressure has been applied at all due to the
thinnest paper being used or for some other reason.
Therefore the shading of handwriting must be analysed as a separate issue. Specimens (35) and (36)
indicate heavy and light shading without pressure
respectively. The positive and negative qualities
associated with this group are given below:—

Character traits (Pastiness)

Positive qualities   Good living
Warmth   Colour influences
Impressionability   Sensuality
The ability to absorb shock   Enjoyment
Naturalness   Humour

36: Shading of handwriting. Sharpness. Pressureless·
Male. Aged 32. Artist. Designer. Model maker. Flex-
ible. Highly sensitive. Intelligent. Sociable. Im-
patient. Intensity of thought experience. Idealism.
Striving for perfection. Very practical. Very aware
of atmosphere. Accurate. Analytical. Leadership.
Problem solving abiiity. Awareness. Kindness.
Analytical and probing mind.   Group B

Negative qualities
Crudeness
Strong sexual urges
Lack of spirituality
Brutality
Excesses
Anxiety
Roughness
Susceptibility to temptations
Materialistic trends
Desire to accumulate possessions
Desire to live on luxurious scale
Pomposity
Lack of overall discipline

Character traits (Sharpness)

Positive qualities

Restraint and reserve

Asceticism

Spirituality (regardless of level this can be
  advanced)

Speculativeness

Intensity of thought experience

Sensitivity

Refinement

Very susceptible to atmosphere and environment

Artistic

Could have feminine trait

Idealism

Emphasis on logic

Sense of discrimination

Negative qualities

Resentment

Pallor of thought

Narrow scope of available experiences

A form of remoteness

Isolation

Anxiety. Inner fears linked to security

Criticalness. Scepticism

Malice

Inability to really enjoy life

Detachment

Need to be understood

Difficulty in finding marriage partner

Touchiness. Could be hurt

Rigid attitude in discussion

8. Width and narrowness

WE are able to observe on sight handwriting which appears to be expansive. Somehow it flows across the page. It emphasises a form of freedom. There is also the type of handwriting which appears to economize on space and is in consequence a narrow form of script. Every writer however has his own particular way of filling up available space.

There are two formulas whereby we can assess width and narrowness. The first is when we take as a 'norm' a letter from the middle zone—such as 'n' where the height of the downstroke is $^1/_8$th inch (or 3 mm) and if the width is equal to the height we can term the letter as being of medium width. Should the width exceed the height of the downstroke by 1 or 2 mm or more then we term the letter as broad. Likewise if the width is less than the height of the downstroke we term the letter narrow. In more simple terms, wide script is where the distance between the downstrokes is larger than the height of the downstroke; and narrow script is where the distance between the downstroke is smaller than the height of the downstroke. Both these formulas are used as a gauge but the best method is still that of impact, whereby one can say without any measurement that the handwriting is either wide, narrow or normal. The private dossier will prove of great value in the early stages of making assessments.

Usually one finds with wide handwriting that the upstrokes tend to become emphasized and with narrow handwriting the downstrokes are emphasized. Wide handwriting is closely associated with the rightward slant, and it is in this direction that the graphologist must look; although the proportion of upright handwriting coming into the wide grouping will be noticeable it is more likely the link itself between wide and normal. The leftward slant is more likely to fall into the narrow grouping. Specimens (37) and (38) indicate wide and narrow handwriting respectively. The positive and negative qualities associated with these groups are given below:—

Character traits (Wide)

Positive qualities
With heavy pressure
Expansiveness
Ambition
Frankness
Demand for a wider living
Elan
Initiative
Forcefulness
Boldness
Self-possessed
Sociability
Extroversion
Striving
Goalmindedness
Slight impulsiveness
Extroversion

Negative qualities
With heavy pressure
Lack of consideration
Lack of social inhibition
Recklessness
All out attitude
Inability to delay
Lack of discipline
Lack of self-control
Inconsiderateness

With light pressure
Broadmindedness
Tolerance
Imagination and vision
Spontaneity
Zeal

With light pressure
Carelessness
Impatience
Adventurousness
Unscrupulousness
Superficiality

Character traits (Narrow)

Positive qualities
With heavy pressure
Restraint
Self-control
Reserve
Moderation
Tactfulness
Self-consistency
Considerateness
Discipline
Inhibition

Negative qualities
With heavy pressure
Inhibitedness
Over-cautiousness
Distrust
Jealousy
Calculation
Deceit
Cunningness
Egotistic
Meanness

With light pressure
Timidity
Modesty
Self-contained
Cautiousness
Slowness
Reasoning

With light pressure
Uncertainty
Anxiety
Neurotic inhibitions
Fear of life in general
Narrowness of views

have not an English
equivalent of Roland — only
I don't suppose out exists —

37 (above): Wide handwriting

Female. Aged 28. Film and T.V. Production. Independent. Alive. Active. Bold. Imagination and vision. Good judgment. Deals with pure essentials. Initiative. Logical. Critical. Good co-ordinator. Quick grasp of facts. Constructive outlook.

Group B

38 (below): Narrow handwriting
Male. Aged 43. Engineer. Practical, realistic, analytical and probing ability. Problem solver. Striving. Immature for age grouping. Balanced. Slight reserve. Non-leader group. Useful for analytical work of practical nature.
Group C

9. Forms of connection

THE original method of writing words was in printed form. Also with the advent of the printing press, valuable and useful as it was, it nevertheless had a further influence on writing whereby people being fascinated by the *regularity* of the printed characters then tried to imitate them. *Good writing* was then interpreted as the best reflection of the printed word and in so doing all individuality was lost; in fact some people endeavoured to print exactly as the printer's press.

The linking of letters by up and down strokes was found not only to increase the speed of writing but it produced fluency and spontaneity. Although this was a developed practice of linking letters by strokes it was found that subconscious thoughts also produced linking strokes: a form of weaving together of letters and therefore a *natural* development rather than a *cultivated* development.

For the purpose of graphological assessment we take four *basic* forms of connection :—

a. The Garland

b. The Arcade

c. The Angle

d. The Thread

*in painting and
to know, if you
in her writing a
thing you the
this page as I*

39: Garland connection
Female. Aged 22. Secretary/Linguist. Independent.
Warm, friendly, kind, sincere, natural. Shows
empathy. Ease of social contact. Sympathy,
womanliness. Easy going, hospitable. Artistic. Can
design fabrics. Weaving.   Group C

The garland

This is one of the most practical and natural forms
of linking middle zone letters together. It is quick,
fluid and allows for ease in writing. The formation is cuplike. It will be observed that the downstroke on touching the base line of the middle zone
then commence its upstroke in a smooth graphic
movement; in fact the whole formation of garland
linkage is one of smoothness. Naturally if the
garland is shallow the writing becomes more rapid,
but still there is the easy flow. One senses an effort-
less motion. It connects with such facets in the
character structure as indicated below. Specimen
(39) illustrates the garland linkage.

Character traits (Garland)

Positive qualities

Easy-going nature
Sincerity
Adaptability
Flexibility
Ease of contact
Confidence
Reconcilability
Naturalness
Sociability
Kindness
Sympathetic approach
Rhythm

Empathy
Liberal outlook
Tolerance
Frankness
Humanitarianism
Ability to recognize others
Optimism (Also observe slant)
Sometimes considerable over femininity (in women)
Naturalness
Mildness in approach

Negative qualities

Easily influenced
Lack of discipline
Indetermination
Instability
Laziness
Emotional
Could be fickle
Superficiality
Inconstancy
Lack of firm attitude
Sometime over-confidence
Tactlessness

The arcade

If one can imagine the garland *in reverse* then this is arcade writing. The fact that this is a reverse in graphic motion now allows the graphologist to interpret the handwriting as that of a complete opposite. The formation is that of an arch whereas the garland was of cuplike formation. There is a lack of ease of flow, there is more attention to its formation, more carefulness, the up and down-strokes forming a structure. Such persons who write like this can be very diplomatic and open. Friendliness is usually lacking and is tested carefully before acceptance, there is a tendency to hide one's true thoughts. The writer is usually more alert and watchful and has a good sense of balance. There can be a coolness in the character structure. Specimen (40) illustrates the arcade linkage and the positive and negative qualities associated with the arcade group are given.

Character traits (Arcade)

Positive qualities
Inner independence
Trustworthiness
Artistic sense of proportion
Sense of distance
Sense of form and style
Sense of stable values
Scepticism
Desire to protect
Pensiveness
Meditativeness
Shyness
Cautiousness
Secretiveness
Depth of feeling
Formalism
Impenetrability
Pride

Sense of tradition
Feeling of distinction
Profoundness

Negative qualities
Haughtiness
Inscrutibility
Desire to hide
Could be hypocritical
Could scheme
Intrigue
Insincerity
Affectation. Falseness
Pretention
Suspiciousness
Could lie
Mistrustfulness
Scheming

Please forgive
f you rf you
can let me

40: Arcade connection

Female. Aged 45. Translator. Intelligent. Realistic and practical. Good judgment. Self-sufficient. Business mind. Money motivated. Would accept a challenge. Bold. Proud. Enthusiastic. Good family background. Obstinate. Sceptical.   Group B

41: Angle connection

Male. Aged 26. German. Intelligent. Conscientious. Observant. Persistence. Slight vanity. Independent. Accurate. Could be careful with money. Intuitive and perceptive. Firmness. Could be open on surface but secretive. Deep concentration and analytical mind.   Group B

this spring. I am sot
it is an idea not to b
thank you for the help
remind you of Ikatja,

The angle

It is necessary to make two graphic movements to produce either the garland or the arcade connection, whereas the formation of the angle requires three movements. Such persons using the angle connection like to have things under their own control and to exercise discipline over those under them. They would never refuse to take responsibility or accept a challenge. The willpower is usually very strong and they lack the fluidity to allow change to take place easily. They are usually relentless in their desire to achieve an objective. Such writers can be very fixed in their ideas and outlook—they can be precise and even aggressive. The mere formation of the angle causes one to observe the writing with a feeling that it lacks smoothness and rhythm. This is a very clear grouping to detect, by its clarity and sharpness. It will be observed from specimen (41) how outstanding such handwriting can be.

Character traits (Angle)

Positive qualities

Firmness	Orderliness
Decisiveness	Contempt for an easy life
Preponderance of reason	Inner conflicts
Strictness	Constancy
Disciplined outlook	High degree of resolution
Sternness	Determination
Serious thoughts	Planning mind
Conscientiousness	Direction towards goal
Obedience to duty	Steadfastness
Persistence	Sense of obligation
Thoroughness	Reliability

Negative qualities

Pretentiousness	Suspicion
Punctiliousness	Domineering
Callousness	Avarice
Intolerance	Unyielding
Aggressiveness	Uncompromising
Lack of humour	Rigidity
Slowness	Pitilessly logical
Heaviness	Unsociability
Dissatisfaction	Aim is to reason
Irritability	Lack of humaneness
Excitability	Lack of sympathy

The thread

When letters are joined together by the linking of upstrokes and downstrokes which are outside the clearly defined groupings such as the garland and arcade and when one is aware that the linkage is indefinite and lacks a feeling of clarity we term this "thread". One finds writers who belong to the creative groupings using this threadlike connection; also those who are extremely mature and who may be very versatile. This group is particularly interesting as one finds diplomats, politicians, psychologists, psychiatrists, advanced business men within it. One can accept such writers as being highly adaptable, flexible, imaginative and always having the desire to lead their lives exactly as they would wish without any form of control from outside influences. Intelligence is usually of a wide nature, not necessarily academic, and it is closely interwoven into the character structure and linked to intuition and perception. In this field one looks for the exceptional. Such writers are usually very impressionable and can reflect the moods of others, they can lack stamina and are more inclined to move with these moods, but it is vital for all concerned to allow them the greatest possible freedom to exercise their fluid type of mentality. They usually refuse to accept a mundane attitude. Specimen (42) gives a clear indication of the thread.

Character traits (Thread)

Positive qualities

Readiness for any situation
Creativeness
Foresight
Versatility
Adaptability
Dexterity
Elasticity
Multiplicity of talents
Diplomacy
Writer sees everything and receives impressions
Instinct
Spontaneous understanding

Negative qualities

Destructiveness
Lack of character
Resentment
Envy
Deceitfulness
Lack of conscience
Insincerity
Feminine trend in men
Elusiveness

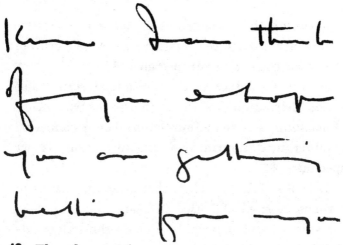

42: Thread connection

Male. Aged 54. Consultant. Flexible. Readiness for any new situation. Vision. Foresight. Imagination. Adaptable. Individualist. Diplomacy. Slight reserve. Instinct. Versatile. Logical. Could enlarge on small matters. Very aware of atmosphere and environment.　Group A/B

Connected or disconnected

The moment we break away from all scholastic impressions and tuition in handwriting, from criticism as to whether our writing was considered good or bad; and allow ourselves the privilege to follow our own inclination as to the method of writing we wish to adopt, then we can truly say that the reflection on paper is that of our inner self.

The method of tuition by various schools throughout the world can be divided into two main groups:–

　(1) Cursive.　　(Running manuscript)
　(2) Uncial.　　(Script)

In the first case, that of cursive writing which is connected and fluid, we accept the connection theory as meaning that in any one sentence at least five letters are connected together into one form of stroke formations, as per specimen (43)

In the second case, that of uncial script, also called 'printscript' we accept the connection theory as meaning *less* than four letters being connected together in one form of stroke formation, as per specimen (44)

It is only fair to explain that although the script form is adopted and used in many schools today, the student will invariably join up the letters (although in the early stages instructed not to do so) *by sheer force of desire and feeling*, so when we come across disconnected handwriting in adult life it still reflects *the desire and wish* to continue in this form from an inner sense: so for the purpose of this chapter we must accept connected and disconnected handwriting as being a *natural expression.*

When writing one has to pause periodically to dot an 'i' or cross a 't' also there is the interruption on syllables in a word. These breaks are considered normal and therefore provided the theory remains concerning the connection of five letters or more, this can be termed connected handwriting. If we observe carefully our writing we will note that the method of connection is through the upstrokes which are very clearly defined in all writing with a rightward slant. These upstrokes could be termed 'bridges' between self (ego) and the outside world. The continuous linking of words by these upstrokes without a break indicates the writers' individual approach to matters of social and intellectual association. They can also indicate logical, continual, and progressive movement towards an objective with the necessary organization and co-ordination. One must carefully note the connection between letters from all three zones. A medium form of connection can be clearly observed under the principle explained. Wherever the writer makes no breaks whatever (that is where even the 'i' dots are linked to letters) see specimen (45), this can indicate a high degree of intelligence and co-ordinating ability.

If all words are linked together without any form of break this is known as *extreme form* and is

43 (above): Cursive. (Running script).
Male. Aged 56. Specialist. Meticulous to detail.
Enthusiastic. Quick grasp. Logical. Good co-ordination. Ability to fight through facts. Purposefulness.
Goalminded. Friendly, sincere, sociable, intellectual
association. Looks to the future. Planning and surveying mind.　　Group A

44 (below): Uncial (Disconnected script).
Male. Aged 75. Clergyman. Highly intuitive. Inventive. Has ideas. Practical and realistic. Marked
vision and foresight. Reserve and restraint. Highly
sensitive to atmosphere and environment. Good
memory. Quick grasp and insight. Psychic sensitivity. Insight into human nature.　　Group A

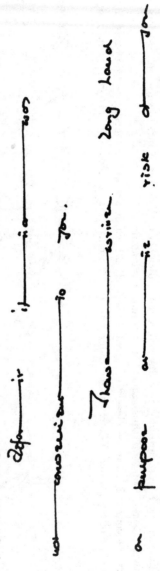

usually written by people who are in a tremendous hurry and whose mental ability towards direction and adaptability is more than normally marked.

One must also observe the clarity of layout in making an assessment. If the writing is rambling one could even detect some form of disorder, as opposed to co-ordination and adaptability, even to the point where there is an overall emotional tendency coupled with excitement. All forms of exaggeration of a particular trend in handwriting must be carefully observed and noted in the dossier.

In the case of disconnected handwriting we can

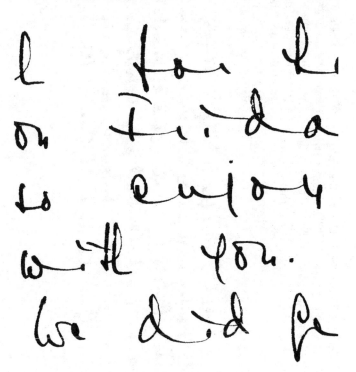

45 (above): The 'i' dot linked with letters
Female. Aged 42. Independent. Bold. Determined. Very marked judgment. Would always accept a challenge. Slight reserve. Realistic and practical. Highly intelligent. Can co-ordinate with ease. Enthusiastic. Energetic. Individualistic.   Group A

have the *slightly disconnected*, and also the *fully disconnected*. In the former case we can have groups of letters in two's and three's making up a word or words, whilst in the latter there is no

46 (below): Slightly disconnected
Female. Aged 42. Market Research Consultant. Independent. Intelligent. Imagination and vision, ideas germinate. Can write. Deals with essentials. Quick grasp of facts. Works a lot on intuition and perception Critical. Sceptical. Has moods. Meticulous to detail. Concentration.   Group A/B

them. I would not offer to help ~ because I believe that it is only will power which can cure people who are affected. In the case of mental health patients ~ I believe that people helping must have a calm and balanced background in order to offset the lack of this in the patients.

connection whatever, see specimens (46) and (47) respectively.

The slightly disconnected handwriting reflects uncertainty and in some cases indecision; it can also indicate the germination of ideas within a limited field. Where there is full disconnection, one enters a group closely associated with individualism, isolation, and a desire to live a separate and detached life. Such persons being highly intuitive and perceptive a very likely to produce ideas and fall within the creative group: one finds inventors, writers etc., within this group.

For the purpose of graphological assessment the positive and negative qualities associated with connected and disconnected handwriting are given.

47: Fully disconnected

Male. Aged 38. Personnel Consultant. Very introverted and conscious of self and reactions of others towards himself. Very sensitive, intuitive. Likes to control his own sphere of influence. Need for praise and encouragement. Can be very secretive. Flexible. Critical. Strong leadership force.
Group A/B

Character traits (Connected) Cursive

Positive qualities
Systematic thinking
Logic
Continuity of thought
Planning
Sense of calculation and strategy.
Reasoning
Deductive thinking
Abstract thinking
Steadiness in work
Theoretical worker
Philosophical
Ability to fight through facts
Need and desire for change
Goalmindedness
Co-operative
Individual approach to matters
Persistence in work
Purposefulness
Social contact and also intellectual association
Practical
Realistic
Comprehensive thinking

Negative qualities
Inconsiderate
Lack of intuitive thinking
Poor observation
Negligence
Restlessness
Tactlessness
Lack of originality

Character traits (Disconnected) Uncial

Positive qualities
Intuitive thinking
Ideas can germinate
Imagination and vision
Inventiveness
Observation and planning
Self-reliance
Intellectual initiative
Quick grasp and insight
Criticalness
Inspirational
Emotional sensitivity

Negative qualities
Inconsistancy
Unsociable
Lack of forethought
Egocentricity
Stubborness
Moodiness
Avarice
Loneliness
Uncertainty
Inner fears
Lack of security
Possible inferiority complex
Lacks adaptability
Possible bad memory
Dislike of criticism
Restlessness
Lack of logical reasoning
Selfishnes
Fearfulness

10. Legibility and illegibility

THERE used to be a time when bad handwriting was thought to denote a bad character and good handwriting a good character; but this of course is not the case; in fact bad handwriting, that is illegible handwriting, can denote a very high degree of maturity; also a complete disregard for whoever has to read it, and a certain disrespect which is hardly ever intentional. The writer is so completely free and unihibited even more so if he writes rapidly; but as long as he can record his thoughts on paper and leave some form of mark he is satisfied. For the recipient it is quite another story, see specimen (48).

This chapter is designed to enlarge on the reasons for legibility and illegibility.

48: Illegible handwriting

Male. Aged 57. Engineer. Active. Intelligent. Flexible, adaptable, vision. Constructive. Sociable. Slight aggression to achieve objective. Would cover himself in an emergency. Concentration. Executive mind. Can control others and take responsibility. Depressed at time of writing. Planning and surveying ability.   Group A

With the advent of the typewriter the illegible writer will indulge as much as possible in this means of conveying his thoughts. He will admire the layout of a letter (because this is usually how he would like to write) and he may openly boast to others that he has 'shocking handwriting'. He will be happy in referring to doctors as belonging to his particular group with a sort of pride as though he was the member of an exclusive club. He will look at clear and distinct handwriting and may remark that it looks 'immature' or possibly 'simple'. The question is why has a legible writer, or near legible writer, deteriorated into an illegible one?

From the educational standpoint one accepts that a person can read and write, and therefore the

49: Legible handwriting

Male. Aged 74. Executive. Diplomatic. Clearminded. Young handwriting for age grouping. Accurate. Careful. Openness. Simplicity of outlook. Knowledge of job. Judgment. Generosity. Patience. Conciseness. Conventional.   Group B education would be incomplete if this were not so. It was originally intended that everyone should write clearly in order to convey thoughts and ideas. Legible handwriting is where every word is clear and readable: only then is it truly legible as per specimen (49).

There are writers who write legibly where every word is not distinct but the text somehow allows us to guess the word which is in doubt. Again we must accept a *medium form* of legibility. One can find in the handwriting of uneducated people great clarity in letter formation, in fact sometimes the most simple (quite apart from spelling errors) write every letter with sharpness which surprises the reader.

It has been said that legible writers show clarity of thought and purposefulness, that school teachers, lecturers, and clergymen all display handwriting that can be clearly read by all: to this we must agree in general, and one must admire this form of handwriting. One can add that legible hand-writing is a form of openness and sincerity, in fact the illegible writer can be condemned out of hand. To counteract this argument we can then produce the handwriting of cultured and intelligent men and women in public life who write illegibly, so therefore we cannot assume that legible handwrit-ing can be a true guide to the mental field of the writer, or an indication of his character being superior to another. Anyone who is involved in work of a detailed nature will strive to perform the graphic style with a sense of artistry. The writer who writes slowly has a better chance of writing legibly than the quick writer, so we find clerical/

bookkeepers, general clerical grades writing with a high degree of legibility.

It would be just as wrong to down grade the legible writer as immature and ordinary, as to up-grade the illegible as mature and sophisticated. One thing is certain, those who are in work requiring meticulousness to detail are more likely to present a clear and uniform script. Also psychologically a writer wishing to convey some form of communication wants to produce the same impression, as if he were in verbal contact. Open and clear handwriting can almost *on the surface* impress the reader with the feeling that the writer wishes to hide nothing, there can even be an indication of simplicity, but it is most important to stress that other factors are involved in the analysis made by the graphologist, and will be explained in a later chapter which can and will alter the whole situation on the factor of legibility and illegibility.

If we take only one point—the forger—here the writer belongs to the legible group—criminals who write from prison more than often have a very open script which is easy to read. One of the most difficult problems a graphologist has to face is giving an opinion on honesty or dishonesty. If the answer was based *purely* on legibility and illegibility a very inaccurate answer would be given.

From the specimens given one has a clear idea of the two types of handwriting and the following information may be of assistance in making an analysis at this stage.

Character traits (Legible)

Positive qualities
Sincerity
Purposefulness
Culture
Talent
Carefulness to detail
Clear thinking
Patience
Desire for clear communication and understanding
Definiteness
Conciseness
Sometimes conventional
Desire for honest dealings
Straightforwardness

Negative qualities
To appear open
Lack of inspiration
Lack of deep education
Pettiness
Inability to cope with difficult problems involving
    depth of understanding
Dishonesty
Lacking maturity
Lack of essential vision and foresight
Living in narrow world
Naivete
Gullible

Character traits (Illegible)

Positive qualities
Reservedness
Living in world of own ideas
Maturity
Secretiveness. Confidential
Desire to be individualistic
Desire for freedom of action
Not conforming to set pattern
Ability to understand others
Sensing
Intuition and imagination
Flexibility
Adaptability
Executive temperament

Negative qualities

Carelessness	Arrogance
Unco-operativeness	Suspicion
Inconsiderateness	Mistrust
Bad manners	Neurotic fear
Insincerity	Confused state of mind
Unpunctuality	
Indolence	
Haughtiness	

11. Capitals

THE very word 'capital' can influence our thoughts. There is a feeling of strength, greatness, a central point; therefore when we refer to or think of a capital letter either consciously or subconsciously we can reveal some of the esteem we hold for ourselves in this one particular letter. Also in the English language we have extracted the single letter

'I' from the alphabet—as an indication of self. Other countries such as Germany with the word 'ich' and France with 'je' and the Latin 'ego' and the Slavonic 'ja', can never truly convey the sharp and direct tone of the one single letter: so therefore particular attention must be paid to the formation of this letter when making a graphological analysis. Capital letters can take on their boldest form in the signature—or the initials before the surname—or at the beginning of a paragraph; but wherever the capital letter occurs, it is most important to pay particular attention to its size and shape as here is the reflection of many facets in the character structure. We can divide this group into large, medium and small, and the following information gives a broad outline of possible characteristics. See specimen (50) indicating large formation.

Large

Where the capital letter extends itself well into the upper zone—and possibly out of proportion to the other letters—this is an indication of a person who not only has a high opinion of self, but feels often superior to others, with considerable pride and a demand to take authority and to be recognized by others. Also it can indicate an idealistic and perfectionist trend, also self-confidence, forcefulness, egotism, vanity, social prestige, ambition, in fact the range of variations in the character structure have been summarized separately for easy reference.

Medium

Balanced handwriting according to the zones reflects an objective evaluation of self, therefore the capitals show no over—reflection and are termed normal.

50 (above): Large capitals

Female. Aged 53. Business executive. Highly active. Ambitious. Pride in achievement. Pride in self. Dignity. Farsightedness. Expansive personality. Enterprise. Boldness. Desire for greatness. Would dislike being overlooked. Leader type. Logical. Vanity. Impressed by wealth and position. Could be jealous of others. Desire to impress.

Group A

112

51 (below): Small capitals
Female. Aged 27. Secretary. Reserved. Flexible. Enthusiastic. Sympathetic. Understanding. Intelligent. Good educational background. Impartiality. Executive ability. Studious mind. Serious outlook. Can underestimate self. Can have lack of confidence. Insecurity. Energy channeled into thinking. Conscientiousness. Modesty. Original outlook.

Group A/B

I was delighted to
hand you letter.
Yes, I have been
posted to Manchester for
2 months, to be followed
by 2 months in London
first, then in time in
London. It will a

Small

Small or exeedingly low capitals can reveal modesty, humility and simplicity. In very ordinary hand-writing they can represent a lack of force, timidity, lack of self-confidence and even a negative personality. As in the case of large handwriting the various variations have been summarized for easy reference. See specimen (51) where the capitals are more or less lost and can hardly be identified.

Character traits (Large)

Positive qualities
Ambition
Pride in achievement
High regard for self
Self-respect
Idealist
Dignity
Farsightedness
Diligence
Self-esteem
Expansive personality
Formality
Enterprise
Boldness
Not afraid to accept a challenge
Some times religiousness
Taste for art, music or poetry
Desire for greatness
To be observed
Would dislike being overlooked
Sense of honour

Negative qualities
Vanity
Self-display
Impressed by others who
have wealth and position
Desire to be greater
Pretentiousness
Conceit can be very marked
Boastfulness
Vanity and exaggeration
Affectation
Desire to dominate
and have own way
Could be difficult
Bad taste
Could show off
Desire to impress
Arrogance
Feelings of grandeur

Character traits (Small)

Positive qualities

Concentration
Reserve
Love of detail
Scrutiny of everything
Conscientiousness
Modesty
Impartiality
Executive ability
Energy channelled into thinking
Studious mind
Critical form of thinking
Objectivity
Concentrated brain group
Matter of factness
Can specialize
Economy
Tolerance
Power to assimilate facts
Spirituality
Mental subtlety

Negative qualities

Pettiness
Lack of confidence in self
Feelings of inferiority
Submissiveness to gain a point
Could get despondent
Lack of enthusiasm
Avarice
Overscrupulousness
Pedantry
Fussiness
Depression

12. Initials and terminals

As we look at a blank piece of paper before writing, the whole space is normally there for us to use with a sense of freedom. We have so far discussed margins, capital letters, the way we tend to fill a page: in fact how to paint the word portrait for others to read. It may be that we have only to write a small note, or leave a message, or we may have to write a statement. But whatever the situation is, the first part of a word is known as the *initial stroke* and the ending of a word the *terminal stroke*. At school we were shown clearly how to start a letter but now away from tuition we have our own method and ways of beginning and ending. The graphologist must watch for these commencing and ending strokes particularly at the beginning of a sentence or paragraph, and where there is often no previous connection with another word. It is in fact the start of a new impulse—a new thought—and therefore the writer is free to move his pen in any way he feels either consciously or subconsciously.

One must look to see whether a starting stroke is used or not. In the first instance we should look for the initial stroke which may be attached to a capital letter—the long stroke can indicate pride, deliberation, slight indecision and possibly less self-assurance than may be indicated from external appearance. People who are dealing with considerable detailed work necessitating careful consideration are inclined to use starting strokes, particularly clerical workers. When the initial stroke is *well below* the base of the letter in question, whether it be a capital or small letter, one can assess the writer as being someone who could have a bad temper, be obstinate, sometimes self-opinionated and unreasonable in an argument. See specimen (52)

It is interesting to note our own handwriting and to observe whether we make starting strokes or not. As people mature and become more self-assured the commencing stroke can slowly terminate and almost die off-this can be observed by collecting samples of children's handwriting over a long period. If a child hardly ever makes an initial stroke and starts off with a clear formation, the intelligence is usually very well advanced, although in some cases it is not an academic intelligence but a quick overall perceptive grasp of facts and information. In the case of adults who use no initial stroke they usually belong to the quick active groupings who have no doubt in their minds as to what they are going to write, there is a very marked forthrightness indicated. They are usually people who direct or who cannot be bothered with detail and who want to 'get on with the job' and to cut out any form of delay or deliberation. Men are more inclined to cut out the initial stroke than women unless the woman is concerned with business affairs and could be termed within the executive class. If one is to observe the handwriting of a normal housewife who is laden down with details, the initial stroke can often be clearly seen and is a good example.

Terminals

It must be understood that the initial stroke takes the full weight of the mind—it is the beginning of something new, in this case, a word. The thought involved is to complete the word, either quickly or slowly, very little thought is being applied to the

...would 'phone me Sometime
...leave the date
...Meantime She thoroughly enjoyed
...The short while you were here, I
...hopes to see You again Soon.
...much love wishes from mother

52 (above): Initial stroke

Female. Aged 39. Executive. Energy, vitality and willpower. Logic. Individualism. Vision, foresight and imagination. Realistic and practical. Highly analytical and probing. Bold. Would accept a challenge. Leader type. Generous. Independent. Slight bad temper. Can solve problems. Strong business temperament. Intelligent.

Group A

53 (below): Terminal stroke

Male. Aged 51. Postman. Marked generosity. Simplicity of outlook. Lacking essential overall maturity. Clearminded. Inquiring and inquisitive mind. Meticulousness to detail. More diplomatic than friendly. Introverted. Analytical mind. No bad temper or aggression. Deals with essentials.

Group C/D

end letter, it has to be terminated by any letter in the alphabet according to the word; and the placement of this letter and the way we terminate it can give some very clear indications of the character structure of the writer. See specimen (53).

Certain letters such as 'e' give us important clues as to whether the stroke is cut short, indicating possible meanness, careful husbanding of personal resources, business mind etc., or whether the stroke is graceful and long, sometimes even sweeping upwards whereby this indication shows the generosity of the writer to give out. Sometimes such writers who show excessive 'giving' are very useful in the business/sales field or with Public Relations, where entertaining is vital and there must be a spontaneous outflow. Where a stroke ends with an abruptness, this can often be seen on 'y' endings—here one can often find curtness and rudeness and a tendency to be self-opinionated. Very thick endings with bluntness can indicate resentful and even sadistic tendencies. Although this book is not intended to give hints to possible forgery investigations, it is strange how many forgers make a mistake on the initial and terminal strokes, either omitting them altogether or enlarging them out of normal proportions.

13. Loops

THE subconscious mind is somehow drawn towards the making of loops which are in various forms linked to our emotional force. The alphabet has provided us with such letters as:—

b   d   h   k   l   and   t

all of which enter the upper zone.

Also it has provided us with such letters as:–

g   j   q   y   and   z

which enter the lower zone–the letter–'f' as we have already observed in a previous chapter can enter all three zones.

The upper loop

In graphology one must observe how the writer forms his upper loop. Should all loops entering the upper zone be long, and obviously ascending toward a height greater than twice the size of the small letter in the middle zone, we can assess the writer as belonging to the idealistic and perfectionist group, who would show strong leanings towards culture of some form coupled to vision and imagination. In such cases where the writing almost climbs towards an unknown point and there is an obvious striving, we can trace strong spiritual leanings. The letters especially to watch in the case of long loops are in the following order:–

l   h   b   k

See specimen (54)

Special note on 'd' and 't' loops:
The letter 'd' can often have a loop inserted–likewise the letter 't' as per specimen (55); where such loops appear we can trace vanity and conceit within the character structure; and the need for praise and encouragement, either from a parent, husband or wife or an employer.

54 (above) : Upper loops
Female. Aged 42. Observant. Watchful. Desire to control. Problem solver. Flexible. Meticulousness to detail. Planning and surveying disposition. Deep concentration and probing. Nothing accepted on the surface. Idealistic and perfectionist trends. Money motivation. Clearminded. Calculation and strategy. Ease of manner. Slight confusion. Goal-mindedness and enthusiasm. Here one sees the upper and lower zones very clearly defined.
Group B

55 (below): Special loops on letters 'd' and 't' Female. Aged 38. Director. Artistic. Bold. Determined. Independent. Can be very secretive. Clearminded. Idealistic yet very practical. Likes to have things under her own control. Enthusiastic. Very hard worker. High opinion of self and justified capabilities. Probing and analytical mind. Original. Need for praise and encouragement.

Group A/B

Just as in the loops which adopt the ascendency so we have loops descending well below the base line in the letters:—

g   j   q   y   and   z

Here where the loop is wide and there is considerable pressure upon the pen, one notes strong sexual forces, strength connected with outdoor sports, students of nature and naturalness. Should the loop be within the group without over-pressure from the pen, then the writer belongs to the realistic and materialistic group; one finds in this group business men—executives, production executives, highly analytical and probing types, those who will accept nothing on the surface. Should the loop open wider at the central point—a broadening formation—one can connect the writer as belonging to the psychological field of research. See specimen (56). Where a loop is wide and long yet has the tendency to go backwards in a leftward slant—here one can trace strong links with a mother influence. This can also indicate a suspicious nature and the desire to withdraw and to analyse quietly, the feeling to avoid any form of conflict.

Loops that are well developed in both upper and lower zones

Where it is obvious that the loops show marked balance, one notes the strong idealistic and perfectionist trends coupled to imagination and vision linking to the practical and realistic trends in the character. In such cases one can find in the writer enterprise and self-confidence and what one could term a 'normal' personality. Should the formation be well balanced but in moderate form then the writer shows stability, interest and initiative and is well aware of normal day to day procedure; there could be a lack of outstanding ability but nevertheless he is a most useful person to work in a team.

Loops which vary in direction

Wherever the loops take on varied directions one can assume that there are signs of inner conflict. This can be linked to emotions caused by atmosphere and environment or a struggle between the idealistic and perfectionist trend and basic materialism. Refer to previous specimen (23).

56: Lower loops

Female. Aged 37. Market Research. Highly analytical. Money motivated. Watchful. Good vision. Flexible and adaptable. Striving. Vanity and conceit trends. Practical. Enthusiastic. Looks to future. Not static. Impatient but thoughtful. Sociable. Diplomatic and friendly.

Strokes instead of loops on letters of normal loop formation

In such cases the writer is expressing his willpower, his firmness and determination and is more inclined to concentrate than to analyse. He can be very practical, also obstinate and hard to convince if the pressure is very heavy. See specimen (57).

Loops that are obviously short in development

Upper. There can be a lack of imagination and vision also any form of idealism or spiritual development is limited and not understood.

Lower. In this case there can often be some form of physical weakness and lack of deep probing. Limited range only.

A *combination* of the above is quite rare as per specimen (58).

57 (above): Strokes instead of loops

Male. Aged 46. Director. Firmness and tenaciousness. Drive. Planning and surveying mind. Intuition. Logic. Deep concentration. Practical. Will take responsibility. Strong leadership. Wide background experience. Not afraid to make and take decisions. Group A

58 (below): Lack of upper and lower loops
Female. Aged 27. Secretary. Deals with pure essentials. Realistic. Enthusiastic. Very factual. Clear thinking in concrete way. Works on strong intuitive force. Idealistic and spiritual trends lacking. Group A/B

14. Introversion and extroversion

WE have all come across the person who is shy, or the person who seems to avoid direct 'eye contact'. At one time such persons were considered deceitful, untrustworthy and even dishonest. Employers when interviewing looked across the table at the prospective employee and made a careful note that he did not look at one directly. Graphology has played a considerable part in dispelling this myth by bringing to the notice of an employer in the graphological report that the person is an 'introvert'. Someone who looks into himself and analyses the reactions of others towards himself.

A very simple theory has been developed which centres round two outstanding letters:—

    (1) 'w' (This is the primary one to look for)
    (2) 'd'

Introversion can also be shown in the backward slant; but the letters 'w' (also the capital 'W') and 'd' give a very quick indication when looking at handwriting, see specimens (59) and (60)

It appears when the end stroke of the 'w' turns *inward* or where the 'd' instead of finishing on the end stroke *downward* also turns inward or backwards. Both these trends indicate introversion to the graphologist. Should the handwriting be of a rightward slant and these letters appear with this inward formation—the writer is then an *introverted/extrovert*. If there are variations in the formation of these two letters—some turned in and some normal—then we can assume that the introversion is partial. Where the 'w' turns *outward* and the 'd' has normal ending then the writer is in the *extrovert group*. Special attention should be paid to children's handwriting. Where the introversion trend is showing, by using the eyes continually with the child this tendency can be eradicated gradually. The positive and negative traits closely associated with introversion and extroversion are as follows:—

Character traits (Introversion)

Positive qualities
Analytical
Imagination
Attention to detail
Methodicalness
Orderliness
Patience
Carefulness
Reflectiveness

Negative qualities
Self-consciousness
Self-analytical
Shyness
Lack of confidence
Sensitivity to atmosphere and environment
Inhibited
Could worry inwardly

Character traits (Extroversion)

Positive qualities	*Negative qualities*
Self-confident	Carelessness
Friendliness	Impatient
Sociability	Could overlook details
Enthusiasm	Quickness in making decisions
Warmth	Impulsiveness
Active	Lack of planning ability
Persuasive	Recklessness
Sales ability	Lack of organizing ability

Then we'll have to contact all the film people we can lay our hands on. The other business was renewed with the real estate. Business for Aquila. We are arranging a meeting for the middle of next week, and I hope we bring it off. We tried in vain to

59 (above): Introversion. 'w' indication
Male. Aged 38. Consultant. Independent. Sensitive. Highly introverted. Ideas germinate. Desire to lead and work on own. Would dislike being controlled. Here the introversion is very marked due to background experiences.
Group A/B

60 (below): Introversion. 'd' indication

Female. Aged 34. Canadian film producer. Very alert. Flexible. Individualist. Reserve. Accuracy. Intelligent. Can adjust herself to new situations. Deals with essentials. Here the introversion is also partially indicated with the 'w'.

Group A/B

15. 'T' bars and 'i' dots

"DON'T forget to cross your 't' s and dot your 'i' s". How many times have we heard these words? In particular the 'i' dot, which is *separated completely* from the letter stem—suspended as it were in the air—causing us to pause in our writing either to go back to place it in position; or we pause at the 'i' to place the dot.

Absence of 'i' dot

Some people prefer never to stop to dot the 'i' at all but go on undisturbed completely omitting all dots from the script. Subconsciously we *know* that a dot should be applied and the letter therefore could be considered – and is – unfinished. Such persons who ignore the placing of a dot have many subconscious reasons for doing so, such as indifference, laziness, impatience, lack of respect for the reader, not considering it necessary. But like everything else in life, once discipline is dispensed with, a habit can be formed, which in this case can produce forgetfulness in other directions. In fact the lack of the 'i' dot can indicate that the writer is forgetful and great care must be exercised in examining such writing for other factors which could give a lead to this trait in the character structure. Any omitting of the 'i' dot must be considered a bad and not a good point when one is making the analysis.

The 'i' dot joined by fluid line connection to next letter or word

Some writers (those who are mature and who are rapid in thought and where in most cases they possess a very good intelligence) have a habit of placing the dot after, either completing the word or letter, and then continuing by a fine or fluid stroke a form of connecting link from the dot to the next letter or word. This can indicate considerable organizing and co-ordinating ability; and the method both being quick and spontaneous presents no delaying factor in the graphic motion. This method usually comes about quite naturally and is seldom adopted; in fact it is hard to train people to do this and still write in a natural manner unless the *feeling* to do so comes from the deep subconscious and is part of the natural graphic movement in an upright or rightward direction. Where such connection is made between the 'i' dot and the first letter of the next word we can establish intuition, constructiveness, planning, deductive form of thinking, vision and foresight. See specimen (61). If the 'i' dot connects itself through this method with the end letter of a word, one notes organizing ability and integration. The positioning of 'i' dots is most important to note and to establish at the commencement of an analysis, as they can indicate the degree of caution, the inquiring and inquisitive mind, the accuracy, the drive etc., as will be observed from the following chart.

Explanation of 'i' dots shown on chart

It will be observed when studying graphology that 'i' dots can take on many forms. In some cases they can be drawn as small circles which would indicate that the writer has a desire to be different from others, often one finds architects and designers using this symbol; they can appear as dashes due to the speed of the writer, but in whichever form they appear, it is necessary for the purpose of assessment to group 'i' dots into three specific categories based firstly on the slant position of the 'i' and secondly whether the dot is in a *low position*—that is near the top of the stem—or in a *high position*—away from the stem. The first position indicating the writer to be more in the realistic, practical and down to earth group and the second indicating the writer to be more in the planning, surveying and inquiring group.

The following explanation of the various categories will give some idea of how the assessment is made.

61: 'i' dot connections

Male. Aged 48. Engineer. Wide vision. Imagination. Constructiveness. Planning. Deductive thinking. Wide scope of available experience. Goalmindedness. Non leader type yet can command respect.

Group A/B

i DOTS

Group 1

	1	2	3

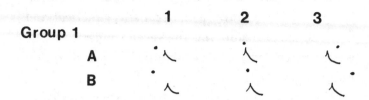

Group (1) A   Dots in low position   Leftward slant

A 1

We must accept the fact that the stem of the letter 'i' is already belonging to the reserved group of writers with a natural cautionary trend. When the 'i' dot is on the left side of the stem, the cautionary factor is increased. So we assume in such a case that the writer is *extremely* cautious, its low position indicating the writers *practical trend*.

A 2

Still in the reserved grouping with the 'i' dot now immediately above the stem in the low position. This indicates caution, reserve with care to detail in the practical sense. This can also indicate a retentive memory. Little imagination is indicated.

A 3

In this case where the 'i' dot is now on the right side of the stem, the indication is that the writer who is basically cautious and reserved shows a desire for action and movement and this now links with a drive force. We can assess the writer as a reserved person who displays action and enthusiasm and has a practical trend and inclination.

Group (1) B   Dots in high position   Leftward slant

B 1

The stem position is still in the reserved grouping but the 'i' dot is now in a high position above to the left of the stem. This indicates an inquiring and

inquisitive mind which can be linked to planning
and survey, but extreme caution is indicated before
any move can be made. Such persons are more than
normally inquiring, in fact they can be assessed as
being highly advanced in this field, even to the
point of nosiness.

B 2

The position of the 'i' dot is still as high as in B. 1
above but it is directly over the stem. This indicates
accuracy, marked inquiring and inquisitive mind,
planning and surveying ability, imagination and
vision. The degree of caution is less in this case.

B 3

The 'i' dot is still in the high position but is now
on the right side of the stem. Here the indication
is that the writer although reserved basically shows
marked movement in the planning and surveying
field, and the inquiring and inquisitive mind is
now enhanced linking with imagination, vision and
action.

Group 2   1   2   3

A

B

Group (2) A   Dots in low position   Upright slant

A 1

We must accept the fact that the stem of the 'i'
is now in the upright position representing those
who belong to the independent and judgement
grouping. Therefore the position of the 'i' dot in
this case simply indicates a practical and realistic
trend and by reason of being on the left side caution is displayed without reserve.

A 2

With the 'i' dot now directly over the stem in the
low position the writer is assessed as highly accu-

rate, realistic and practical exercising marked judgment. One finds often in this group accountants, system analysts and programmers, personnel officers and those on work study.

A 3

With the 'i' dot now moved to the right side of the stem action increases, still within the practical field coupled to judgment, independence and realism. In this group one often finds persons working on new techniques where speed, accuracy and judgment are a vital combination. Often it will be found that the 'i' dots are mixed with A. 1 and A. 2.

Group (2) B   Dots in high position   Upright slant
B 1

Again the inquisitive and inquiring mind comes to the fore by the placement of the 'i' dot to the left side of the stem in a high position. Here very marked cautionary vision is displayed, as though the writer who is basically independent and displays judgment is holding back and reserving his decision.

B 2

The 'i' dot is now directly over the stem of the upright 'i'. Still within the inquiring and inquisitive group but the survey being made is completely co-ordinated. The planning mind is now poised for action which is tempered by the basic judgment factor.

B 3

Now the 'i' dot has moved to the right position. Here we get the combination of judgment, independence, inquiring and inquisitive mind linked to planning and survey—and *movement*. This is the final stage where the writer has such a combination of positive qualities that such men find positions in production planning based on long term projects.

Group 3

	1	2	3
A	*ı*	*ı*	*ı*
B	*ı*	*ı*	*ı*

Group (3) A Dots in low position Rightward slant

A 1

The rightward slant is automatically one of movement and adaptability. The low position of the 'i' dot in this case to the left side has little major effect on the overall movement; it can act as a form of brake but very little more. The writer is a man of action and movement and it is possible that this 'i' dot which indicates caution in the practical and realistic sense, just allows him that measure of delay necessary before things move forward.

A 2

Now the 'i' dot is directly over the stem and by its very position it moves forward in line indicating considerable accuracy, realism and positiveness. This is the indicator of balanced movement.

A 3

This is the maximum point that the 'i' dot will move ahead of the rightward slant. This indicates impatience, restlessness, a desire for extreme action, goalmindedness, a propensity for new enterprises, marked realistic and practical adaptability. Most executives indicate these trends.

Group (3) B Dots in high position Rightward slant

B 1

Again the 'i' dot moves into the leftward position. Once more the inquiring and inquisitive mind comes into action coupled by movement and adaptability. Here is the linkage between action and planning, the 'i' dot is in a cautionary position almost as if it were looking down on the whole situation which is going forward and carefully observing without delaying speed.

B 2

Centring itself now directly over the stem the 'i' dot moves forward automatically with the inquiring and inquisitive mind linking itself with accuracy and exactness. The planning and surveying ability is well co—ordinated.

B 3

Once more the 'i' dot moves to the right of the stem. This time the indication is one of *forward vision*. Such persons are able to see far ahead, realize possible contingencies, be able to warn of approaching difficulties, this possibly is the supreme position of the 'i' dot — so small yet playing such a part in the overall assessment of graphology.

This section may appear rather lengthy—but it is known that the 'i' dot has its own distinct position to play in building up the overall word picture.

'T' bars

The 't' bar can be used with either the capital or the small letter 't'. Its positioning is of vital importance in regard to such factors as leadership and the control of others. Should a short 't' bar be used, one can assume that there is some form of timidity and perhaps a lack of confidence, such a person can be very well balanced but can lack the dynamic thrust. There is also the person who produces a 't' bar which if another 't' is being used will continue the stroke in a form of bridge. Such persons are considered the natural problem solvers and are highly valuable in all branches of commerce and industry etc., see specimen (62)

Should the writer omit the 't' bar from his letter he is in the same position as the writer omitting the 'i' dot—perhaps impatient, not accepting responsibility, a person of impulse with a lack of real objective; drifting. Or on the other hand it could represent a writer who is rather unconventional and not conforming to a set pattern and who considers himself to be different from others.

It must be accepted that there are possibly more than fifty variations in the type of 't' bar used, as will also be observed from the specimens in this book, but like the 'i' dot it is necessary for the purpose of assessment to place them in the following groups as per chart and explanation.

Explanation of 't' bars shown on charts

Although the chart outlines eighteen different types of 't' bar, as already mentioned there are possibly more than fifty variations deriving from this basic source, it is therefore considered that the summarized information below will cover the broadest possible outline when carrying out graphological assessments. The stem of the 't' must be associated naturally with the various slant positions.

t BARS

	1	2	3
Group 1			
A			
B			

Group (1) A 'T' Bars in left position Various slants

A 1

The position of this 't' bar is possibly at its lowest point, also it will be observed that it is on the left-hand side of the stem, indicating that the writer is a person of caution, uncertainty, procrastination, could suffer from depression, inferiority feeling and lack of essential drive and zest.

A 2

The 't' bar in this case is now raised to a middle position but still on the lefthand side of the stem. The cautionary factor whilst still there is moderated likewise other factors mentioned above in A. 1.

A 3

This is now an extreme position in relationship to the 't' bar in A. 1.

The indication here is more interesting and advanced as it concerns the field of leadership whereby the writer by using a 't' bar at the top of the stem emphasizes his leadership inclination whilst at the same time is hesitant to use it fully.

Group (1) B 'T' Bars in left/right position Various slants

B 1

Again the 't' bar is at its lowest position, indicating on one side caution but the desire to overcome it; such persons adopt a cautionary and steady attitude, lack forcefulness, self-confidence, but slightly overcome feelings of inferiority and procrastination.

B 2

The 't' bar in this case shows a very balanced position and is quite common; such persons whilst cautious are still able to go forward but without a dynamic thrust, showing marked conscientiousness and attention to detail.

B 3

Again an extreme position in relation to B. 1. Here one notes leadership with caution, the desire to control, to be recognized, a tendency to seek something which could be unobtainable.

Group 2

	1	2	3
A			
B			

Group (2) A   Short 'T' Bars in right position touching stem   Various slants

A 1

Again we are entering a low position but the cautionary factor has now lessened, but the writer indicates timidity, possible lack of confidence and even underestimation of self. He could be reluctant to take responsibility and prefer to hold a subordinate position.

A 2

This can be assessed as the 'middle course'. Could be very conventional, conforming to pattern, lacking the dynamic, but nevertheless in advance of A. 1. above. Would take on limited responsibility in a narrow field exercising conscientiousness, diligence, carefulness, orderliness etc.,

A 3

Due to the 't' bar reaching the top position one is aware of leadership, not the dynamic form but that where considerable care is exercised, consideration of others, no domination, openmindedness and adaptability to control within limited range.

Group (2) B   Long 'T' Bars in right position touching stem   Various slants

B 1

Although the 't' bar is in a low position the obvious extension of the bar indicates the ability to take on greater responsibility, at the same time exercising protective measures to those coming within the orbit of control or in contact with; the long 't' bar connects with the same group shown in specimen (62) those possessing problem solving ability.

B 2

The 'middle course' in this instance shows an ever increasing tendency towards responsibility, problem solving, control and protection of subordinates, goalmindedness, vision and foresight. Such persons although not born leaders nevertheless accept responsibility readily.

B 3

Where the 't' bar in this instance takes the top position, one not only finds leadership potential but the overall ability to accept control and to administer with fairness, correctness and with empathy. One finds stability, ambition, the natural problem solving ability, vision, foresight and imagination coupled to planning.

Group 3

	1	2	3
A	t	t	t
B	t	t	t

Group (3) A   Long and medium 'T' Bars detached from stem   Various slants

A 1

The very nature of the movement in this case brings the 't' bar into a higher position at the commencement. It is seldom as low as in Group (1) B. 1 and Group (2) A. 1 and B. 1. Such persons are those of movement and activity, enterprise, and where thoughts run ahead of action, they will accept challenges, are prepared to meet new projects and are stimulated by other's ideas, in fact even in the lowest position one is always confident that the writer will never stagnate.

A 2

All the attributes mentioned above are increased by the higher position of the 't' bar — in substance they are the same but with greater tenacity, zeal and drive; also there is a greater desire to control the situation. Goalmindedness is very much in evidence, coupled to speed and sometimes considerable impatience.

A 3

Here we reach the highest point again. Leadership and the desire to control completely. Impatience not only with self but with others being directed. Essential that the writer is in a position of complete authority and is given freedom of action. All the attributes outlined in A. 1 and A. 2 are incorporated with the main facet, that of leadership. Such writers are in the minority but are of the utmost value in any field where essential control is required

Group (3) B   Long and medium 'T' Bars detached from stem in upward direction   Various slants
B 1

Where the 't' bar is in a raised position or upward direction which is very obvious and can be seen clearly in specimens (1) and (7), the desire to dominate and control is very much in evidence and such persons try to use their will over others, although not fully in the born leader group, as will be seen in Group (3) A. 3 and Group (3) B. 3, they nevertheless feel the power of leadership and can take over most difficult situations demanding control. Not always easy to get on with, for there is a tendency to *demand* more than to *request* and a very firm attitude can result which can at times

144

cause friction with those in a subordinate position.

B 2

Here is an emphasis on B. 1 above. Demand is greater. Control is stronger. This midway point which is so near to full leadership causes the writer to enter the highly ambitious groupings, the tendency is to get ahead at all cost, usually there is impatience and a demand for recognition and respect. They are persons essentially of control and have the ability to see ahead and to direct others towards the objective. They are not always easy to get on with on account of the demanding tendency, but with a high intelligence rating the will gain the necessary respect due to them.

is not too good. I think Attitude to our marria not sound (though he would no doubt be nes and she needs someou her the way. Perhaps I help.

62: 't' bar connections

Male. Aged 51. Specialist. Co-ordination. Directness. Problem solving ability. Secretiveness. Firmness. Meticulous. Active. Energetic. Would accept a challenge.

Group A

Here is possibly the highest point where leadership is associated with the 't' bar. Its raised position and detachment from the top of the stem automatically brings the writer into the field of administrative executive control—this can be seen in specimen (52) of a woman executive: here the 't' bars are even higher than those shown on the chart. Such persons embody the inborn and natural desire to control and lead and with high intelligence and belonging to Group A in regard to form level have the capacity to encompass the maximum field of operations in their respective spheres.

16. Types of ink used

TODAY we use colour tests in the selection of personnel, where the results of these tests give a broad but identifiable outline of the character structure. The significance of colours in our daily life has long been the subject of research with regard to the important part it plays in the human aura, the effect on our thoughts and on our emotions and temperament. Just as we choose our pen—so we choose our ink. This is a well established fact. The development of various shades of blue ink over the last fifty years is a very noticeable feature of our writing habits, and the manufacturers have made a special study, not purely to increase sales, but to meet a real and positive demand by the public, which is of an aesthetic nature and has a very strong connection with colour psychology. Therefore the colour of the ink used by a writer (also the type of paper) can give some very reliable information as to certain traits in the character structure, and such information must be incorporated in the overall general analysis of the handwriting. The general range can be covered by the following colours—blue, black, red, green, with subsidiary colours such as violet, watery black etc., below is given a summary of an evaluation made over a long period on various specimens of handwriting.

Blue

The whole range of blue is considered to have a strong connection with inspiration, harmonious understanding, matters of a spiritual nature, religion, loyalty and sincerity.

Blue black

Used by a person with a business mind. Usually fairly masculine, normal, conventional with no desire to be exceptional or to influence the reader that he is different or outstanding from others. This can be termed a universal colour.

Blue

Here one enters a more adventurous field. Often this type of ink goes with blue notepaper. There can sometimes be femininity in the male who uses this colour, also masculinity in the female. There is a desire to impress slightly. It is an enthusiastic colour and there can be a considerable link with people of an artistic temperament.

Royal Blue

Here is a colour that in itself is happy to look at. It is a joyful colour and seldom does the writer seem to suffer from depressions in his handwriting. Without doubt the writer is *drawn* to choose this colour, it is not by accident, but by design and desire. Women (especially those who are moving in society, and those who feel that they belong to the affectionate group known as 'mums') seem to delight in using this type of ink. It can also link with certain femininity in men, and again masculinity in women.

Black

There are various shades of black, from the deepest shade to the watery variety; but it is considered a serious colour in complete contrast to the blue series mentioned above.

Black/Very dark: Brown/Pale

The bolder type of writer uses these colours, sometimes with a wide pen nib. One finds students, draughtsmen, designers etc., using these colours, also business men who are either going to make their mark or have already done so. These are a strongly impressionable colours and are meant to be noticed. They indicate power and force. Without doubt considerable seriousness toward life in general is displayed.

Black/Watery pale

Here the same impression is sought but often the pen used is of a thinner type and the writer often belongs to the artistic grouping. Writers, musicians, poets show a preference for this colour. Again we get seriousness and sometimes depression indicated in the handwriting. Without doubt a considerable number of writers belong to the hypersensitive groupings.

Red

The colour red is always accepted as the symbol of life, strength and vitality. It is connected with ambition, generosity and also affection. Can have strong links with the physical.

A colour that used to be outstanding for various reasons. In business circles such as in banking it is used with frequency, this in turn often causes executives to continue using the colour. One must not overlook possible pomposity, or the 'know all' type. Schoolmasters, lecturers, accountants, lawyers, all have a desire to use red. It is a professional colour to just give that shade of difference with the 'masses'. A desire subconsciously to be different. One finds most of the writers in upper groupings.

Green

Generally considered to be a symbol of harmony, adaptability, versatility, with mental development extending beyond the normal.

It has been found that most writers using green ink have indicated a desire to be different. There can be links with an inferiority complex, where writers belong to the medium or lower groupings or where there is something in the personality which detracts and the use of green ink supplies a certain 'want' which causes others to be conscious of the person who uses this colour. One finds young people using this particular ink − also those who may be connected with the artistic field ie., art, music or literature.

17. Envelopes

THE very first impression we get possibly of handwriting is the name and address written on the envelope (if it is a letter) or on a card. It is important never to destroy the envelope and specimens should be retained in the dossier. Although we are not going to use the handwriting on the envelope for analysis purposes we are going to watch how the writer *places* the name and address of the addressee.

Although the letter may be written illegibly or in a great hurry the writer is nearly always careful to see that the envelope is clear and distinct; in fact it could be said that the greatest legibility is on the envelope. Although the post office complain of indistinct adresses, lack of postal district numbers, insufficient information, actual leaving out of streets, even towns, however incorrectly the envelope is written, much can be learned about the writer's disposition.

The clear thinking person who has organizing ability, balance and judgment will use the centre position of the envelope and carefully space out the name and address of the person concerned. One finds, with writers who have studied calligraphy, that tremendous care is taken to produce a first class word portrait of the address; again this is the outward expression of orderliness and care. The very natural writer continues to write the address on the envelope in the same handwriting as the letter, and any major difference between the handwriting in the letter and the envelope can be interpreted on size and slant and other factors explained in the analysing procedure. One thing is most important to watch continually and that is the *positioning* of the address. If we assume that the centre position

63: Lefthand top corner
Male. Aged 63. Manufacturer. Independent. Sensitive.
Analytical. Realistic and practical. Can make social
contact. Sales.

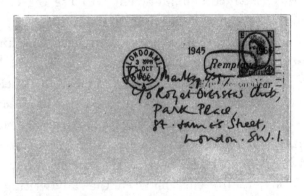

64: Upper right-hand corner
Female. Aged 42. Flexible. Adaptable. Independent.
Meticulous to detail. Good organizer. Highly ob-
servant and watchful.

is the correct and accepted position, then any alteration from this point must have a meaning. We have already ascertained that handwriting in a leftward slant position belongs to the more reserved group than that in the rightward slant position; and therefore if the address is written in the *left-hand top corner* one notes first the inquiring and inquisitive mind, detachment, lack of confidence and more than normal reserve. There is also a form of breakaway from realism into a possible fantasy state of thinking. Such writers quite unknown to themselves adopt this form of addressing of envelopes. See specimen (63).

If the address is in the bottom left hand corner—this represents the basic realistic field. Here the materialistic influences are strong and this can cause, from the withdrawn position, such factors as envy, suspicion, caution and doubt about others, but above all—suspicion. It is interesting to note that there are more envelopes addressed at the *bottom left hand corner* than the top. See specimen (66).

Having dealt with the left hand side of the envelope we now proceed to the right—here an entirely new situation arises. The desire for independence, freedom, release from restriction, the vision and foresight, the looking ahead—all is displayed in the positioning.

It is more convenient to write in the *lower right-hand* corner on account of the stamp position but this seldom detreacts the writer from choosing his position. Again we enter the materialistic field, the desire for freedom which is based on a strong materialistic footing. There is a desire for the writer to

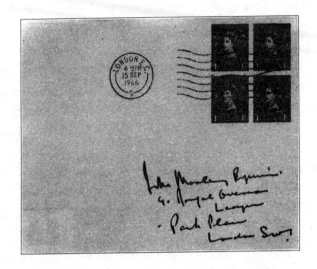

65: Lower right-hand corner
Male. Aged 54. Consultant. Slight reserve. Idealistic.
Deep concentration. Generosity.

66: Bottom lefthand corner
Female. Aged 21. Student. Academic. Judgment.
Active. Uninhibited. Obstinate. Striving. Diplomatic. Sense of humour.

release himself from past environmental experiences. There is no feeling of illusion; all must
be on a firm basis. See specimen (65).

When the address is placed in the *upper right-hand
corner* there is the same desire for freedom, release
from restriction, the vision and foresight, the looking ahead, but the basis in this case is not connected
with materialism to the same extent—it is more the
desire for uncontrolled freedom where the person
can express himself without fear of the conse-
quences. There can be strong idealistic and perfectionist tendencies involved. See specimen (64).

If we look back on previous chapters it will be
observed that the slant positionings and their meanings have a close resemblance and relationship with
the address placement on envelopes. It is considered
a good idea to correlate the information obtained
from the envelope with that of the contents if this
is possible.

18. The importance of the signature

QUITE apart from our normal handwriting our
signature holds a distinct place in the field of graphology. In these modern times with the ever increasing use of the typewriter, the signature may
be the only specimen of handwriting we have to
work on and although more difficult to analyse
than a few lines of handwriting, it is in fact perhaps the most intimate piece of graphic movement
to be ever recorded on paper. It is the accepted representation of self on all documents, cheques,
credit cards, driving licences etc., in fact wherever
we have to *testify* to our identity this small piece of

handwriting is well and truly ourselves. The fact that we often use our signatures and that the repetition of its useage produces a natural fluidity presupposes that much can be learned from its formation. It is strange how this *conscious* form of handwriting of which we are so aware of as we sign represents our own idea of ourselves and our relationship with others and how we hope others will see us. The signature can develop naturally, but more often than not it is produced by a method of practice to see if we 'like it' or whether it is a 'good looking signature' or for some other reason. Children have a tendency to copy their signatures many times and as they get older they begin to

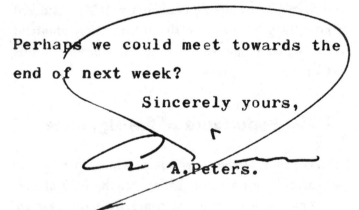

Perhaps we could meet towards the end of next week?

Sincerely yours,

A. Peters.

67: Original signature

Male. Aged 43. Market Research. Advertising. Here one notes the thread connections, the very high loop, the speed. Originality. Readiness for new situations. Foresight. Idealistic and perfectionist trends.   Group A

establish something which *appeals* to them—perhaps they have observed their parents signatures or someone elses, and they have a sense or feeling to copy. There is the 'original' signature—something quite outstanding—which bears no relationship with the overall handwriting structure, and which is formed mainly to create some impression or to over-emphasize self; but whatever the reason, the writer displays a form of double nature, or shrewdness, a self-centred outlook and a high opinion of self, putting up a front. But the graphologist can still detect the basic dominants in the character structure which will appear also in the handwriting; so in fact there is no true way of disguising oneself from the graphological analysis, but on the surface to the ordinary layman the signature may bear no relationship to the handwriting. The so-called 'original' signature, as per specimen (67) is an exception to the rule that most signatures do bear a relationship to the normal graphic movement.

Once a signature has been established as conforming to our inner desire, it seldom changes throughout life, other than where normal maturity is involved and the signature takes on a very natural fluid and mature pattern, but never loses its original identity. It is accepted that a signature which shows no difference to the script indicates the writer to be a natural and unpretentious person who in both business and private life adopts the same behaviour and manner. There is an indication of equipoise and an even nature, an an unconcern for self, a complete naturalness and lack of self-consciousness. There is no effort to put up a front or veneer. Such writers can at times be self-complacent and can be objective when considering their own faults and virtues. See specimen (68).

68: Similarity of signature with script

Female. Aged 58. Executive/Press. Here one notes the complete naturalness of the handwriting. Directness, clarity and forthrightness. No pretence or veneer.   Group A

" The Vicar? "

" Yes, he told me to cut the legs off the bed! "

All for now As ever *Scrolling*

69 (above): Signature smaller than script
Male. Aged 39. Sales director. Outwardly very extroverted. Temperamental. Impulsive. Alive. Signature
shows genuine modesty and a dislike of boasting.
Group A/B

70 (below): Signature larger than script
Female. Aged 20. Student. The handwriting has a certain simplicity. Dominant parents have always overshadowed the girl. Now at university the true force of personality emerges. Desire to be recognized and to come into her own sphere of influence.

Group B

Detaching ourselves from the writer whose signature is *completely* identified with the handwriting almost as a continuous pattern, we now come to the variation groupings which are listed as follows:—

Where the signature is smaller than the script

In such a case the writer is more modest than he demonstrates, it is as though he is assuming a role in life which is not a genuine expression of himself. Such signatures illustrate mildness, forcelessness, lack of concern with other people's opinions of himself, self-deprecating, servility, and sometimes even a lack of overall dignity. There can be a deliberate attempt to represent himself to others as an inferior; this can link with a protective measure. In most cases like this, one finds that the writer belongs to the sensitive grouping and may feel that he should never fully show his true potential. Should the writer belong to the introverted group there can also be strong inferiority influences submerged. See specimen (69).

Where the signature is larger than the script

The reverse situation now occurs. Here the writer is more self-reliant in her private sphere than she is inclined to demonstrate openly. In young men and women who display considerable ambition this can indicate the potential. One can detect pride, forcefulness, and the desire to be recognized as an important figure. Should the signature be overlarge, this can indicate false pride and pretentiousness. See specimen (70).

Where the signature has a leftward slant with a rightward slant script

The writer in this case makes an attempt to repress her normal affectionate and sociable nature. There is a form of brake applied to natural responsiveness. A domestic problem can cause this to happen or where there is an unnatural atmosphere. It can also mean that the general outwardness or extroversion is only used for effect and there is really a natural reserve in the character structure. The writer could build a form of reserve and restraint in order that she can adjust herself to a certain situation. This type of signature is rare and if found should be placed in the dossier with as much information on the writer as possible. Can be inner conflict in such a case. See specimen (71).

71 : Signature with leftward slant with rightward script

Female. Aged 44. Continental background. Intuitive, accurate, ideas. Can be easily hurt. Constructive and logical. Openly friendly but in private life very reserved. Depressions and uncertainty.

Group B/C

72 (above): Signature with rightward slant with leftward slant script

Male. Aged 37. Manufacturer. Very reserved inwardly but in the sales field on impact very extraverted and progressive. Can solve problems. Need for encouragement. Analytical. Good concentration. Good planning capacity.

Group B

73 (below): Signature with flourishes

Male. Aged 32. Estate Agent. Independent. Resents any interference. Enthusiastic. Likes to put on 'act'. Could be actor. Vanity and conceit. Sensitive. Slightly nervous disposition. Involved within himself. Likes to be in the limelight.

Group B

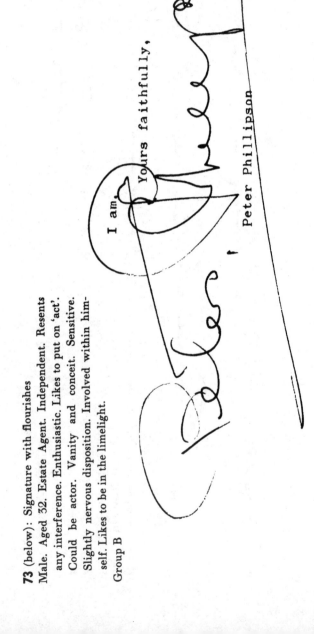

I am,

Yours faithfully,

Peter Phillipson

12, Great George Street, Westminster, S.W.1.

Yours faithfully,

74: Signature underlined

Sex unknown. Age unknown. Although this is the signature of a firm, it is nevertheless indicative of a person who is optimistic, bold, showing pride, diplomacy, constructiveness and observance. Someone who takes responsibility.

Group B

Where the signature has a rightward slant with a leftward slant script

Here the writer wishes to present a warm and affectionate front, in fact this is a form of veneer and it can apply to very demonstrative and effusive persons who are actually very unemotional. It is usually a very clever and careful person who uses this method of signature and they can often be associated with those who carry out schemes of a secretive nature. One is never completely sure in such a case and therefore special attention must be applied when carrying out the analysis with the knowledge that the main characteristic is reserve and the external behaviour is very much a cultivated act. In this case there can also be an inner conflict: See (72).

Where the signature has flourishes

When the signature is elaborate and the flourishes are outstanding one can expect some form of ostentation, vanity, love of display, and a desire to attract attention. Should the flourish take on a lasso-like form then the writer indicates a very self-assertive nature with a desire to keep things under his own control and with a resentment against anyone who interfered in his life. See specimen (73).

Where the signature is underlined

Writers who are firm and determined and who take responsibility and who have a justified sense of importance will apply the under score of a signature. Sometimes it will be the whole length of the signature, or appear just at the end with an extension beyond the signature, in all cases this is a sign of taking responsibility. See specimen (74).

IN the previous chapters we have traced a certain path towards an objective, in order to find a simple method to use whereby we can start to analyse handwriting; and achieve a reliable word picture of the character structure of any particular writer. In one section of this book we have talked about 'i' dots and 't' bars, we have talked about 'capitals' and 'loops' and as no handwriting is ever alike there must necessarily be within the alphabet of twenty-six letters many variations in the formation of the individual letters. This chapter is to cover such a situation.

We must accept that our early teaching at school brought about a rough outline of how we write to-day: should we have remained *static* our writing would look childlike, but due to our having *matured*, our handwriting has either improved, deteriorated, or has taken on many facets never taught at school. We can *add* new elements to the letter formation, or we can *take away* by a form of economizing. Somehow we have been able to write and make ourselves understood despite these alterations that we have made individualistically; and it would be fair to say that any *simplification* in the letter form would indicate that the writer is able to see the pure essentials, to be objective and purposeful and differentiate between the important and the unimportant. In fact he is able to dispense with the unnecessary.

On the other hand the writer who has *added* to the letter formation by flourishes, upward lines, loops and hooks etc., is unable to cut out the unimportant and is more inclined to ponder and lack the ability to differentiate and see things in a clear light; but there is the more aesthetic sense in the character structure in comparison with the writer who has simplified his writing into practical form. Therefore we can accept that simplification is a form of measurement of the writer's intellectual maturity, culture and taste.

For the purpose of graphological assessment we divide letter formation between simplification, as per specimen (75) and amplification, as per specimen (76). The positive and negative qualities associated with these groups are given below:—

Character traits (Simplified)

Positive qualities
Concentration
Intelligence
Objectivity
Philosophical frugality
Creativeness
Practicality
Maturity
Cultural pursuits
Self-abnegation
Mature pondering
Sense of dealing with essentials
Thoughtfulness
Simplicity of outlook
Clarity
Sense of order
Directness of approach
Insight
Wisdom
Mental power to weigh and to judge
Sense of reality and observation

Our interests are diverse — I am not-very
keen on Xenopus or bufo bufo but
prefer the toads of _____. Admittedly, re
are only to a small extent models of
an environment, but (T do th).

Comparison of the development of Xenopus laevis with
those of _____ known to be an interesting study. At first
the chief difference to be noted are in the methods of

75 (above): Simplified letter formation
Male. Aged 50. Female. Aged 52. Husband and wife.
Here one notes the balance and the compatibility
also the simplified forming in both cases of the
letters.

Group A

76 (below): Amplified letter formation
Female. Aged 44. Here one notes the amplification of
letters very clearly. The flourishes and additions,
the complications and lack of overall clarity.

Group A/B

Character traits (Amplifications)

Negative qualities
Reserve
Lack of social contact
Tactlessness
Lack of appreciation of
    anything that does not
    serve a purpose in life
Lack of sense of beauty
Lack of sense of tradition
Neglect
Insincerity
Coldness
Ruthlessness

Negative qualities
Bad and vulgar taste
Vanity
Boastfulness
Posing
Affectation
Pomposity
Cumbersome
Complexities in outlook
Vain exaggeration
Desire to 'show off'
Over emphasis on formality
Eccentricity

Positive qualities
Taste for decorative forms of presentation
Taste for effects and arrangement
Form sense
Pride and formality
Cultivation of details
Originality
Sense of representation
Urge to create an original atmosphere
Ability to smooth and to reconcile
Living in the past. Tradition
Desire for traditional living
Desire to live in colourful atmosphere

If we were to extract every variation of every letter in the alphabet known to graphology we would require a special book to give the explanations, and therefore as this book is only a preliminary to the subject it would be inadvisable to give

anything other than the most salient small letters
to observe which are as follows:—

a   Should the small letter 'a' appear
to be written larger than other
letters in various words—should it
appear to 'stand out'—as in specimens (2) and (10) the writer is
inclined to be jealous.

a   Should the small letter 'a' be clos-
ed with a loop formation at the
top the writer can be secretive.

a   Should it have a double loop formation—and this can be seen in
the word 'float' the third word
down in specimen (33)—this indicates a combination of both exaggeration and secrecy, the forward loop being the exaggeration
section, this can appear on its
own in the word 'have' under
specimen (40).

b   If the letter 'b' is written without a loop as in specimen (1) indicated in the word 'before' the
writer is an individualist.

f   If the small letter 'f' has a reverse loop formation in the lower
zone as in the word 'helpful'
under specimen (23), the writer
shows calculation and strategy.

g   Should the lower loop present a
'triangle' formation as per specimen (40) the writer shows—obstinacy.

j

Again, the 'triangle' formation as per specimen (41) indicates—obstinacy.

y

Also under the same specimen (41) the 'triangle' formation appears again indicating—obstinacy.

k

If the small letter 'k' is enlarged and out of proportion to other letters as in the word 'thank' in specimen (11) this is a reliable indication that the writer has a tendency to enlarge on small matters out of proportion to their true worth. Under the same specimen it will be observed in the word 'week'.

o

If the small letter 'o' has a loop insertion at the top of the letter—as in the letter 'a' already mentioned—the writer also belongs to the secretive group. See specimen (33) the word 'focus' third line down.

o

The double loop formation involves both exaggeration and secrecy. See specimen (33). The word 'tow' sixth line down.

Method of making an analysis

No two graphologists ever work completely alike in their method of producing a graphological analysis; and therefore it would be wrong to establish a set formula. Various methods have been applied, all being satisfactory in producing final results; so if we outline some of the basic principles to follow, these can later be adjusted to fit individual requirements. It must be particularly remembered that every character trait is influenced to some degree by every other trait and cannot be judged by itself. In all cases it is essential to obtain the age and sex and nationality of the writer.

One should *relax* and examine carefully the handwriting specimen *without* the magnifying glass to obtain the *overall impression*. Never rush. The first impact is the most important. Never jump to conclusions. Get the *feeling* of the handwriting. The main thing is to *enjoy* analysing. The more specimens you see the better. Never get disappointed if you appear to have made a mistake in the assessment, accept that you are wrong and note where the mistake has been made. Often you can be right but the person concerned (who may be present) who is being analysed may not like to admit to a possible truth which has been brought out by the analysis.

Chapter five of this book has been designed to give you outstanding graphological signs to look for, chapter six has been designed to give you a list of special characteristics in letter formation. If you follow the order given under chapter five from (a) to (s) you can build up the analysis this way by using the *character traits* shown under the various sections where the positive and negative trends have ben summarized. From this information you can devise your own system of working.

It is important to retain either the specimen of the handwriting submitted for analysis or if you have to return it have a photostat copy made for reference purposes. You should use a form for analysis work similar to the one shown opposite.

Some graphologists work on a permanent fixed principle of analysis, and although this is excellent and brings about a uniformity, one is inclined to get into a rut; and therefore it is suggested that each specimen is viewed with renewed interest. Parts of the handwriting may be used as 'high points' which strike one forcibly on impact.

It could be that one is immediately impressed by leadership and organizing ability, or that the quality of judgment may stand out, or boldness: in fact every specimen produces some *outstanding characteristic*. If one is going to have a fixed set of principles they can take on various formations.

System (1)
Movement
This will cover size, slant, direction of lines, initials and terminals, organization and co-ordination trends, rhythm, speed and shading.

Form
This will cover individualistic or original handwriting, flexibility, form level, connected or disconnected script, loops and again overall rhythm.

Layout
Slant, spacing, margins, positioning of handwriting into zones. Rhythm. All 'i' dots and 't' bars.

Some character traits will appear to overlap under the above system but by careful blending of the positive and negative qualities outlined, a word picture of the character will be built up in detail ready to be put into report form.

System (2)

Margin. Size. Slant. Spacing. Direction of lines. Pressure. Speed. Width or narrowness. Form of connection. Connected or disconnected. Legibility or illegibility. Capitals. Initials and terminals. Loops. 't' bars and 'i' dots.

The above systems can be used as a basis for the overall analysis. It is however considered more important that the method of working out an analysis is devised by the graphologist himself; for it is this freedom of expression and method that produces the best results and opens up new avenues of thought. One realises over a certain period of working that there is a definite pattern forming which produces results which are proved satisfactory. In whatever way these results are being achieved, standardization of method is not recommended.

A specimen analysis has been extracted as an example and every effort will be made to explain the method adopted in this case.

The specimen of handwriting submitted was not written especially for the analysis—so therefore maximum naturalness can be accepted.

The correct age and sex has been given.

The graphological analysis form on the facing page has been used.

Only the positive and negative qualities shown

ANALYSIS OF HANDWRITING

REFERENCE

DATE

NAME

ADDRESS

AGE

SEX

NATIONALITY

SPECIMEN SUBMITTED

SUBMITTED BY

DATE SUBMITTED

ANALYSIS

under the various character traits in this book have been used.

The analysis has been accepted by the person concerned as accurate.

Specimen analysis

Confidential.	Reference: L/G/474/MN
	6th June 1964.
Name:	Code (1)
Address:	London.
Age:	44.
Sex. Male:	Group A.
Nationality:	British.
Specimen sub-mitted:	One letter dated the 31st May 1964 containing approximately eighteen lines of handwriting. Also for comparison purposes a letter dated 19th March 1963 has been used containing approximately thirty lines. Biro type pen.
Submitted by:	Code (1)
Date submitted:	3rd June 1964.

See specimens on pages 178 *and* 181

The writer in this instance is essentially a person with *vision and foresight*, highly *capable, intelligent* and displaying *energy*, vitality and willpower, coupled to tenacity, *determination* and endurance. It should be noted that he belongs to the *leader group*. It is vital that he is given *freedom* of action, also *praise and encouragement*, in order that the leadership quality can thrive and be used to its fullest extent. One notes the need for the writer to have space for himself, he could not lead a cramped existence, and in many ways he could have the desire to live a life on a fairly large scale. The natural qualities of pride, *independence*, generosity, *enthusiasm* are very much to the fore in this case, also noblesse, *self-reliance* and the faculty for long term planning. The present specimen of handwriting submitted shows *restlessness*, *impatience*, *considerable thoughtfulness*, *concentration* and the desire for change. One notes throughout the handwriting a secretive trend whereby the writer can keep much to himself whilst appearing open on the surface, this links with work of a confidential nature which could or has at times surrounded the writer. He could be very reliable. He is very susceptible to atmosphere and environment and has the ability to assess others. Being of a positive mind himself with inborn leadership qualities he would not suffer fools gladly, neither would he tolerate indecision. The writer shows considerable ambition and would accept a challenge and take full responsibility for his actions, he would also be able to delegate work to others with the full knowledge of their ability to perform the task allotted, this is linked to a probing and analytical mind and to intuitive and perceptive qualities. The writer is essentially an individualist and does not conform to a set pattern, this can sometimes cause a form of aggression and the desire to have his own way, one notes here a submerged bad temper, also slight obstinacy, but these factors can be offset against an extrovert tendency whereby warmth, friendliness, sincerity and kindness more than compensate. The writer is clear-minded, has a quick and active grasp of facts, is realistic and factual and shows

CODE (1)

19 March 63

For the next week or so I
expect to be down here near
Southampton, but I hope that it
will not be long before I get an
assignment near to London which
may enable us to meet.

Sincerely

accuracy and carefulness without destroying the drive factor for getting things done.

In comparing the two samples of handwriting ranging over a year one notes an increase in maturity, slight nervousness as though considerable energy has been released even sometimes to a point of exhaustion, yet the enthusiasm and optimism have not been impaired. It is the *enthusiasm and optimism which are the outstanding features in the handwriting*, the writer could influence others and *inspire others* by his courage. He possesses the faculties of observation, co-ordination, organization, genuineness and spontaneity. He is continually looking to the future, he must have *variety and change* and a sense of purpose, this is connected with his goalmindedness, he sets himself a target and tries to achieve the objective, he would in certain circumstances almost accept the impossible. One must always realise that such persons as the writer are *leaders*, but the writer himself must also realise this, he should use his eyes at all times with everyone, in order to put over the power of his inner personality. He should be encouraged whenever possible to take full responsibility, for on this he will thrive.

Such persons as the writer like to have friends and could seek success and recognition in the social sphere, one notes also submerged emotional variations and there could also be slight vanity and conceit submerged; again this is linked with the necessity for praise and encouragement. One notes affection, warmth, the ability to love, devotion, kindness, self-sacrifice if necessary, adaptability, dexterity, social ease, doing a thing for its own sake, verbal articulateness, communicativeness, curiosity and·an inquiring and inquisitive mind linked to planning and survey. He also shows empathy, helpfulness, unselfishness, goodness, humanitarianism and the ability to adjust to a new situation.

One notes agility, vivaciousness, zeal, interest and initiative, quick intellectual grasp and a richness of inner resources. One notes inner balance, a sense of form and beauty, directness and friendliness and diplomacy combined. Elasticity and adaptability are most marked. One notes also an identification with higher values, idealism and constructive logic, coupled to deductive thinking and systematic work. There is also a sense of calculation and strategy.

Finally, this is a person who shows confidence, frankness, sincerity, naturalness, a readiness to recognize others, he belongs to the leader group and as such should lead. He has an executive mind, maturity, and a depth of background experience, all linked to the necessary vision and foresight to achieve whatever objective is required.

Explanation of method used in this case

Using the analysis form all the preliminary remarks have been entered. In this case we are fortunate in having two specimens of handwriting to deal with and it will be observed that there is a considerable overall change in the handwriting during the period of one year—however the *basic dominants* remain.

Overall impression

First of all it is necessary to gain the overall impression of the handwriting. What is the first thing

31 May 1964

You like to know age and nationality; our aged 24 years and English. If it is possible I would particularly like the analysis to cover those attributes which a friend might be inclined to notice and those which an enemy would see.

Sincerely

that really stands out? The letter of 1964 indicates speed, vitality, aliveness, one can sense the force and drive and the pressure is heavy. Another thing which is very obvious in both letters that is the direction of the lines. So with these three important factors immediately we have something to work on, so we can refer to the positive and negative qualities outlined under:—

    (1) Speed (Quickness)
    (2) Direction of lines (Ascending)
    (3) Pressure (Heavy)

If we proceed further we note that the handwriting can be placed in the middle zone (2) as shown on specimen (15). Also there is a tendency for the handwriting to enter the larger grouping, and further both specimens indicate a rightward slant. So now we are in possession of three more items of information as follows:—

    (4) Zone (Middle)
    (5) Size (Large)
    (6) Slant (Rightward)

If we continue to extract from the positive and negative traits outlined under the various sections headed 'Character Traits'—we can commence to build up the word picture. At this point we note that the handwriting is connected, that it is wide and not narrow, that it is legible and not illegible, that the left hand margin is narrow and the right-hand margin broad and so we can list four more items:—

    (7) Connected or disconnected (Connected)
    (8) Width and narrowness (Wide)
    (9) Legibility and illegibility (Legible)
    (10) Margins (Narrow left. Broad right)

What else can we observe? It is noted that the form of connection is garland, that the 't' bars are at the top of the stem, that the 'i' dots are in various positions, that there are loops in the letters 't' and 'd' indicating as we know vanity and conceit and need for praise and encouragement; also there are no loop endings on the 'y' but short loops on the 'g'. Altogether we have now more than sixteen salient points. One notes that the letter 'b' has no loop formation, indicating individualism, the spacing between the words is wide, the writing is regular, the letter 'w' is open and there is no turning inward on the final stem which could indicate introversion, and so on. This is the method to use. Each analysis should be different in arrangement in order that there is no standardization in making a report. Use the index in the front of the book selecting the most outstanding points that are observed on immediate impact. Continue to build up the private dossier using this book as the foundation for further study and advancement.

Finally, remember that this is a confidential subject and that any information you may obtain during your course of study should always be treated as – confidential.

A PERSONAL WORD FROM MELVIN POWERS, PUBLISHER, WILSHIRE BOOK COMPANY

My goal is to publish interesting, informative, and inspirational books. You can help me to accomplish this by sending me your answers to the following questions:

Did you enjoy reading this book? Why?

What ideas in the book impressed you most? Have you applied them to your daily life? How?

Is there a chapter that could serve as a theme for an entire book? Explain.

Would you like to read similar books? What additional information would you like them to contain?

If you have an idea for a book, I would welcome discussing it with you. If you have a manuscript in progress, write or call me concerning possible publication.

Melvin Powers
12015 Sherman Road
North Hollywood, California 91605

(818) 765-8579

MELVIN POWERS SELF-IMPROVEMENT LIBRARY

ASTROLOGY

BRIDGE

BUSINESS, STUDY & REFERENCE

CALLIGRAPHY

CHESS & CHECKERS

___ CHESS TACTICS FOR BEGINNERS *Edited by Fred Reinfeld*	7.00
___ HOW TO WIN AT CHECKERS *Fred Reinfeld*	5.00
___ 1001 BRILLIANT WAYS TO CHECKMATE *Fred Reinfeld*	10.00
___ 1001 WINNING CHESS SACRIFICES & COMBINATIONS *Fred Reinfeld*	10.00

COOKERY & HERBS

___ CULPEPER'S HERBAL REMEDIES *Dr. Nicholas Culpeper*	5.00
___ FAST GOURMET COOKBOOK *Poppy Cannon*	2.50
___ HEALING POWER OF HERBS *May Bethel*	5.00
___ HEALING POWER OF NATURAL FOODS *May Bethel*	7.00
___ HERBS FOR HEALTH—HOW TO GROW & USE THEM *Louise Evans Doole*	5.00
___ HOME GARDEN COOKBOOK—DELICIOUS NATURAL FOOD RECIPES *Ken Kraft*	3.00
___ MEATLESS MEAL GUIDE *Tomi Ryan & James H. Ryan, M.D.*	4.00
___ VEGETABLE GARDENING FOR BEGINNERS *Hugh Wiberg*	2.00
___ VEGETABLES FOR TODAY'S GARDENS *R. Milton Carleton*	2.00
___ VEGETARIAN COOKERY *Janet Walker*	10.00
___ VEGETARIAN COOKING MADE EASY & DELECTABLE *Veronica Vezza*	3.00
___ VEGETARIAN DELIGHTS—A HAPPY COOKBOOK FOR HEALTH *K. R. Mehta*	2.00

GAMBLING & POKER

___ HOW TO WIN AT POKER *Terence Reese & Anthony T. Watkins*	7.00
___ SCARNE ON DICE *John Scarne*	15.00
___ WINNING AT CRAPS *Dr. Lloyd T. Commins*	5.00
___ WINNING AT GIN *Chester Wander & Cy Rice*	3.00
___ WINNING AT POKER—AN EXPERT'S GUIDE *John Archer*	10.00
___ WINNING AT 21—AN EXPERT'S GUIDE *John Archer*	7.00
___ WINNING POKER SYSTEMS *Norman Zadeh*	3.00

HEALTH

___ BEE POLLEN *Lynda Lyngheim & Jack Scagnetti*	5.00
___ COPING WITH ALZHEIMER'S *Rose Oliver, Ph.D. & Francis Bock, Ph.D.*	10.00
___ DR. LINDNER'S POINT SYSTEM FOOD PROGRAM *Peter G. Lindner, M.D.*	2.00
___ HELP YOURSELF TO BETTER SIGHT *Margaret Darst Corbett*	7.00
___ HOW YOU CAN STOP SMOKING PERMANENTLY *Ernest Caldwell*	5.00
___ MIND OVER PLATTER *Peter G. Lindner, M.D.*	5.00
___ NATURE'S WAY TO NUTRITION & VIBRANT HEALTH *Robert J. Scrutton*	3.00
___ NEW CARBOHYDRATE DIET COUNTER *Patti Lopez-Pereira*	2.00
___ REFLEXOLOGY *Dr. Maybelle Segal*	5.00
___ REFLEXOLOGY FOR GOOD HEALTH *Anna Kaye & Don C. Matchan*	7.00
___ 30 DAYS TO BEAUTIFUL LEGS *Dr. Marc Selner*	3.00
___ WONDER WITHIN *Thomas F. Coyle, M.D.*	10.00
___ YOU CAN LEARN TO RELAX *Dr. Samuel Gutwirth*	5.00

HOBBIES

___ BEACHCOMBING FOR BEGINNERS *Norman Hickin*	2.00
___ BLACKSTONE'S MODERN CARD TRICKS *Harry Blackstone*	7.00
___ BLACKSTONE'S SECRETS OF MAGIC *Harry Blackstone*	7.00
___ COIN COLLECTING FOR BEGINNERS *Burton Hobson & Fred Reinfeld*	7.00
___ ENTERTAINING WITH ESP *Tony 'Doc' Shiels*	2.00
___ 400 FASCINATING MAGIC TRICKS YOU CAN DO *Howard Thurston*	7.00
___ HOW I TURN JUNK INTO FUN AND PROFIT *Sari*	3.00
___ HOW TO WRITE A HIT SONG & SELL IT *Tommy Boyce*	10.00
___ MAGIC FOR ALL AGES *Walter Gibson*	7.00
___ STAMP COLLECTING FOR BEGINNERS *Burton Hobson*	3.00

HORSE PLAYER'S WINNING GUIDES

HUMOR

HYPNOTISM

JUDAICA

JUST FOR WOMEN

MARRIAGE, SEX & PARENTHOOD

MELVIN POWERS' MAIL ORDER LIBRARY

METAPHYSICS & OCCULT

RECOVERY

SELF-HELP & INSPIRATIONAL

The books listed above can be obtained from your book dealer or directly from Melvin Powers. When ordering, please remit $2.00 postage for the first book and $1.00 for each additional book

Melvin Powers
12015 Sherman Road, No. Hollywood, California 91605

HOW TO GET RICH IN MAIL ORDER
by Melvin Powers

1. How to Develop Your Mail Order Expertise 2. How to Find a Unique Product or Service to Sell 3. How to Make Money with Classified Ads 4. How to Make Money with Display Ads 5. The Unlimited Potential for Making Money with Direct Mail 6. How to Copycat Successful Mail Order Operations 7. How I Created A Best Seller Using the Copycat Technique 8. How to Start and Run a Profitable Mail Order, Special Interest Book or Record Business 9. I Enjoy Selling Books by Mail – Some of My Successful and Not-So-Successful Ads and Direct Mail Circulars 10. Five of My Most Successful Direct Mail Pieces That Sold and Are Still Selling Millions of Dollars Worth of Books 11. Melvin Powers' Mail Order Success Strategy – Follow It and You'll Become a Millionaire 12. How to Sell Your Products to Mail Order Companies, Retail Outlets, Jobbers, and Fund Raisers for Maximum Distribution and Profits 13. How to Get Free Display Ads and Publicity That Can Put You on the Road to Riches 14. How to Make Your Advertising Copy Sizzle to Make You Wealthy 15. Questions and Answers to Help You Get Started Making Money in Your Own Mail Order Business 16. A Personal Word from Melvin Powers 17. How to Get Started Making Money in Mail Order. 18. Selling Products on Television - An Exciting Challenge 8½"x11" – 352 Pages...$20.00

HOW TO SELF-PUBLISH YOUR BOOK AND HAVE THE FUN AND EXCITEMENT OF BEING A BEST-SELLING AUTHOR
by Melvin Powers

An expert's step-by-step guide to successfully marketing your book 240 Pages...$20.00

A NEW GUIDE TO RATIONAL LIVING
by Albert Ellis, Ph.D. & Robert A. Harper, Ph.D.

1. How Far Can You Go With Self-Analysis? 2. You Feel the Way You Think 3. Feeling Well by Thinking Straight 4. How You Create Your Feelings 5. Thinking Yourself Out of Emotional Disturbances 6. Recognizing and Attacking Neurotic Behavior 7. Overcoming the Influences of the Past 8. Does Reason Always Prove Reasonable? 9. Refusing to Feel Desperately Unhappy 10. Tackling Dire Needs for Approval 11. Eradicating Dire Fears of Failure 12. How to Stop Blaming and Start Living 13. How to Feel Undepressed though Frustrated 14. Controlling Your Own Destiny 15. Conquering Anxiety 256 Pages...$10.00

PSYCHO-CYBERNETICS
A New Technique for Using Your Subconscious Power
by Maxwell Maltz, M.D., F.I.C.S.

1. The Self Image: Your Key to a Better Life 2. Discovering the Success Mechanism Within You 3. Imagination – The First Key to Your Success Mechanism 4. Dehypnotize Yourself from False Beliefs 5. How to Utilize the Power of Rational Thinking 6. Relax and Let Your Success Mechanism Work for You 7. You Can Acquire the Habit of Happiness 8. Ingredients of the Success-Type Personality and How to Acquire Them 9. The Failure Mechanism: How to Make It Work For You Instead of Against You 10. How to Remove Emotional Scars, or How to Give Yourself an Emotional Face Lift 11. How to Unlock Your Real Personality 12. Do-It-Yourself Tranquilizers 288 Pages...$7.00

A PRACTICAL GUIDE TO SELF-HYPNOSIS
by Melvin Powers

1. What You Should Know About Self-Hypnosis 2. What About the Dangers of Hypnosis? 3. Is Hypnosis the Answer? 4. How Does Self-Hypnosis Work? 5. How to Arouse Yourself from the Self-Hypnotic State 6. How to Attain Self-Hypnosis 7. Deepening the Self-Hypnotic State 8. What You Should Know About Becoming an Excellent Subject 9. Techniques for Reaching the Somnambulistic State 10. A New Approach to Self-Hypnosis When All Else Fails 11. Psychological Aids and Their Function 12. The Nature of Hypnosis 13. Practical Applications of Self-Hypnosis 128 Pages...$5.00

The books listed above can be obtained from your book dealer or directly from Melvin Powers. When ordering, please remit $2.00 postage for the first book and $1.00 for each additional book.

Melvin Powers
12015 Sherman Road, No. Hollywood, California 91605